HIKING
MAINE'S 4,000-FOOTERS

Doug Dunlap

Down East Books

Camden, Maine

To Michael Hohne and Angela Werner,
who encouraged me to put my Maine mountain ramblings into print

Down East Books

An imprint of The Rowman & Littlefield Publishing Group, Inc.
4501 Forbes Blvd., Ste. 200
Lanham, MD 20706
www.rowman.com

Distributed by NATIONAL BOOK NETWORK

Copyright © 2021 by Doug Dunlap
All photos by Doug Dunlap
Maps created by Hohne-Werner Design

Quotation from *The 4000-Footers of the White Mountains* (2nd ed., 2008) by Steven D. Smith and Mike Dickerman, used by permission from Bondcliff Books, Littleton, New Hampshire.

British Library Cataloguing in Publication Information available

Library of Congress Cataloging-in-Publication Data available

Names: Dunlap, Doug, 1944– author.
Title: Hiking Maine's 4,000-footers / Doug Dunlap.
Description: Camden, Maine : Down East Books, 2020. | Includes bibliographical references. |
   Summary: "Maine has 14 mountains over 4,000 feet in elevation. Registered Maine guide
   Doug Dunlap has summited all 14, and he shares his wisdom and experience in this guide, providing
   detailed directions to trail heads, trail routes and difficulty levels, what to expect as you hike,
   and other useful information"— Provided by publisher.
Identifiers: LCCN 2019059542 (print) | LCCN 2019059543 (ebook) | ISBN 9781608936991 (paperback) |
   ISBN 9781608936984 (epub)
Subjects: LCSH: Hiking—Maine—Guidebooks. | Trails—Maine—Guidebooks. | Maine—Guidebooks.
Classification: LCC GV199.42.M2 D86 2020 (print) | LCC GV199.42.M2
   (ebook) | DDC 796.510974104—dc23
LC record available at https://lccn.loc.gov/2019059542
LC ebook record available at https://lccn.loc.gov/2019059543

∞™ The paper used in this publication meets the minimum requirements of American National Standard for Information Sciences—Permanence of Paper for Printed Library Materials, ANSI/NISO Z39.48-1992.

Contents

Caution!

Be prepared to take care of yourself in this strikingly beautiful, rugged terrain—to avoid a mishap and to care for yourself should you have a mishap. Maine trails are not regularly patrolled, with the exception of major routes on Katahdin, and even these, owing to the remoteness and difficulty, are covered in only a limited way.

Many hours—including an overnight—may pass before emergency personnel can be notified and arrive to assist. Have the clothing, gear, water, food, and minimum safety preparations to care for an injured person in the field overnight and in changing weather.

See the suggestions in this book for what to wear and what to bring on your outing. Research other reputable sources of your choice for hiking footwear, clothing, gear, hydration, nutrition, trip planning, and safety information.

It is recommended that every 4,000-Footer hiking party have one or more members who hold a current certification in wilderness first aid. New to outdoor life? Take a course in outdoor skills as these pertain to mountain hiking. Consider a guided hike led by a Registered Maine Guide.

The descriptions herein are good-faith accounts of the author's personal experience. Experiences of others will vary.

Trails and routes in this book cross private property, state parks and public lands, National Park Service lands, land trusts, and property of various not-for-profit organizations, each of which has its own policies and procedures for trail access, maintenance, and oversight.

The possibility exists of the closing of a trail and changes to—among other things—approach roads, trail locations, the nature of a route or trail, services and amenities, and fee structures.

Always inform a responsible person in writing of your hiking plans, when you expect to return, and what authorities to contact in event of concern.

> The author and publisher explicitly state that the user of this book bears full responsibility and assumes all risk for safety. Author and publisher assume no liability for the use of this book, including, but not limited to, accuracy of descriptions of trails and terrain, conditions of trails and approach roads, mishaps or accidents that may occur, or the completeness of lists of suggested items to bring or safety preparations to make.

Before Hitting the Trail

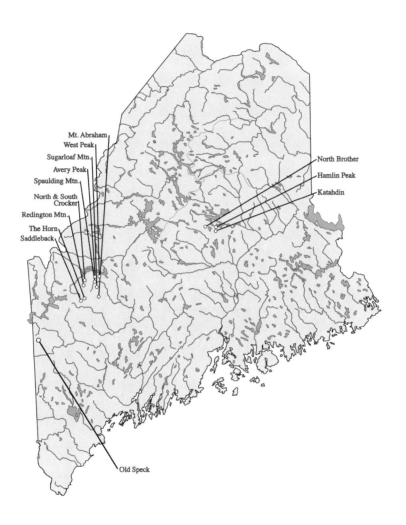

Mt. Abraham
West Peak
Sugarloaf Mtn.
Avery Peak
Spaulding Mtn.
North & South Crocker
Redington Mtn.
The Horn
Saddleback

North Brother
Hamlin Peak
Katahdin

Old Speck

Welcome to the Maine Mountains!

Welcome peak-bagger—or take-your-time hiker, trail runner, or fish-the-ponds-along-the-way explorer! I have written this book to share with you the adventure of hiking amid one of the great wild regions of eastern North America—the mountains of Maine.

I have been hiking the trails of northern New England for decades. On my first day of 4,000-Footer hiking, at age fifteen, I summited Mt. Washington in New Hampshire by way of the Crawford Path. Talk about starting at the top of the list! In the years since, I have summited every one of the sixty-seven New England 4,000-Footers—a good number of them many times.

A love of wild and remote places has carried me to the Colorado Plateau and the Canyonlands of the Southwest, to the Alaska Range, to the Appalachian chain from Georgia to Maine as an Appalachian Trail hiker, to the John Muir Trail in the Sierras, to Pacific Crest Trail sections in Oregon and Washington, to Nova Scotia, and to the Highlands of Scotland. I have led backpacking trips as an Outward Bound instructor, and I am a Registered Maine Guide.

My family and I are fortunate to live in the foothills of western Maine, where the nearest forest walk is outside our back door and into the woods behind our farm home. We have a view of Mt. Blue in one direction and of one of my favorite high peaks, Mt. Abraham (known locally as Mt. Abram), in another.

Introducing people to the joys of exploring our forests, hills, and high peaks and of paddling Maine's ponds, lakes, rivers, and streams by kayak and canoe—this is a joy for me. I hope to see you on the trail!

This book describes every approach trail to each of Maine's 4,000-foot peaks. I have person-ally hiked each trail described in this book—most of them many times.

What to Expect

Roughly 100 miles north of the Gulf of Maine on the North Atlantic and up to 150 miles south of the St. Lawrence River in Canada, the highest of Maine's peaks rise along the northeast reach of the great Appalachian mountain chain, which extends along a southwest-to-northeast cant, surrounded by the great Northern Forest, the largest contiguous forest in the East, in this, the most forested state in the United States.

On a clear day, the view from many of these peaks extends to the Camden Hills and to Mt. Cadillac and neighboring peaks of Acadia National Park, at the edge of the Atlantic, southwest to Mt. Washington and the Presidential Range, and north to Katahdin. Make a way above tree line and discover plant life of the alpine zone—mats of white diapensia and alpine azalea, yellow-flowered bluebead lily, tiny white star-flower, deer's hair sedge and Bigelow's sedge. Join company with bald eagles, Bicknell's thrush, gray jays, dark-eyed juncos, American pipit, or the rare Katahdin artic butterfly. Watch cloud formations shaped by competing winds that slice in from the sea, shoot out of America's heartland, or bear down out of the Arctic—to converge right here, where these peaks rise.

As for those winds, it is their sheer force, and the powerful rains, snows, and ice they bear, that answers the question of how there can be tree lines on peaks only 4,000 feet high. Yes, here is an alpine climate in Maine at that elevation. It is tough for plant and animal and bird life to survive under the harsh conditions. Trees, if they survive at all, are the fabled krummholz—twisted, low-lying varieties primarily of balsam fir, black spruce, and white birch. What endures here is quite remarkable!

As for the rugged nature of the landscape, attribute that to the glaciers that once encased this land in ice a mile deep. As the glaciers retreated, the last of them some eleven thousand years ago, their great force shaped the sharp slopes, notches, valleys, and ravines where hiking trails now pass. In the Northeast in general, and certainly in Maine, major switchbacks are a rarity. Trails tend to go straight up ridges, which renders them short for the elevation gain involved—but steep, requiring a bit more time to hike than one might expect at elevations well below those of the Rockies, the Sierras, or the Pacific Crest.

Here, visionary and dedicated trail crews, most of them composed of volunteers, have laid out, cut, marked, and signed trails to follow to reach Maine's high ground. In the valleys below are trail-supportive towns, maintaining village hospitality while offering meals, lodging, supplies, shuttles, and other hiker services.

The 4,000-Footer Idea

In 1957, in an effort to introduce the growing numbers of the hiking public to mountain terrain outside the popular Presidential Range and Franconia Ridge in New Hampshire, the Appalachian Mountain Club (AMC) created a list of New Hampshire summits at an elevation of 4,000 feet or higher. By publicizing the list and making available recognition of those who hiked them all—the opportunity to become a member of the so-called Four-Thousand-Footer Club (FTFC)—the AMC hoped to spread the hiking community over a broader expanse of mountain country and to introduce hikers to areas in the White Mountains surely worthy of a visit but little known to the hiking public at the time.

The idea had been brewing for some time. In the Adirondacks, the "46ers Club" had formed in 1937. That name came from the number of peaks in the Adirondacks understood to be at an elevation of 4,000 feet or higher. The specific peaks selected for the Adirondack list and the White Mountain list have been modified in the years since the founding of the two projects—in part because of improved measuring techniques.

So successful was the AMC effort that calls came for the inclusion of peaks in Vermont and Maine. In the case of Maine, a familiar objection arose. The mountain terrain in Maine was considered too rugged, and therefore too difficult, for most hikers. That same argument arose when Mainer Myron Avery argued for the Appalachian Trail, slated to have its northern terminus on Mt. Washington, to extend to the summit of Katahdin in Maine. Avery was successful in advocating for the Katahdin extension, and so were Maine 4,000-Footer proponents generations later. In 1964, the New England Four-Thousand-Footer Club added five peaks in Vermont and twelve in Maine.

As a result of new measurement technology, Redington Mountain and Spaulding Mountain in Maine were added to the list in the 1990s, bringing the Maine list to fourteen mountains and the New England total to sixty-seven. (The New Hampshire list added two more peaks, increasing the original list to a total of forty-eight. There are no mountains above 4,000 feet in Massachusetts, Connecticut, or Rhode Island.)

Those who summit all sixty-seven peaks and submit an approved application to the Four-Thousand-Footer Club are invited to an awards ceremony in Boston sponsored by the AMC. The name is added to a FTFC master list, a certificate is awarded, and patches and pins become available to wear. At this writing, nearly twenty thousand people have joined the New Hampshire list and nearly six thousand the New England list.

4,000-Footers in Winter

In response to requests to recognize hikers who ascend 4,000-Footers in winter, a Winter Four-Thousand-Footer Club has been established. Those who complete that task receive appropriate certificates, patches, and pins. The peaks must be summited during the winter season between the winter solstice and spring equinox.

Note that winter conditions (i.e., cold, ice, snow) in themselves do not qualify. The hike must be taken during the above-mentioned calendar period. I once hiked to the top of Saddleback during the second weekend of October in knee-deep snow with snowstorm gusts up to 30 miles per hour—but that did not count as a winter hike for Winter Four-Thousand-Footer Club purposes because it was not in the calendar season of winter.

All of Maine's fourteen 4,000-Footers are "available" to be hiked in winter (i.e., open to the public). However, certain conditions apply in Baxter State Park (Katahdin, Hamlin, North Brother), where a prior application for a permit is required, and certain routes may be closed to hiking. Sugarloaf and Saddleback ski areas historically have required an uphill pass for hikers when open for skiing, as a safety measure.

For all fourteen peaks, prospective hikers must plan in winter for longer access distances compared with other seasons because parking areas and access roads may not be plowed.

In "Out of the Ordinary," later in this book, I provide winter access information.

New England Hundred Highest

The New England Hundred Highest was established in 1967. This list includes the original sixty-seven peaks and the next thirty-three lower summits in New England by order of elevation. Maine has thirteen mountains on this list. Navigation and logistical details are extensive. I mention New England Hundred Highest peaks that are in the vicinity of 4,000-foot mountains—in the event that hikers may wish to conduct further research and hike these peaks.

To summit these peaks, particularly those without maintained trails, requires specific preparations, outdoor skill sets, and wilderness experience. This book should not be considered as a guide to such peaks. Contact the Four-Thousand-Footer Club for directions, maps, and essential preparation information.

Northeast 111

Yet another list is that of the combined 4,000-Footer lists for New England (sixty-seven) and New York (forty-six), established in 1967. Your math is correct: Those figures amount to 113. The original list has expanded to include more peaks, as a result of new measuring methods, but the original name for the list has been kept.

Four-Thousand-Footer Club Rules, Instructions, and Official Lists

Specific rules apply for a hike to qualify for the New England Four-Thousand-Footer Club, New England Hundred Highest, and the Northeast 111. Contact the FTFC (http://amc.4000footer.org).

Hike Your Own Hike

For those who are out to peak-bag, the mountains are calling! Do be aware that there is no single way in which the 4,000-Footer list is approached. Surely the most common approach is to hike one or two at a time, on a day hike. Beyond that, hikers have created quite a variety of ways to tag all peaks—some of them quite novel! Among these:

1. Hike each peak on a separate day. For instance, when hiking the Crocker Range of North and South Crocker, complete two separate trailhead-to-summit hikes, one for each peak, for a total of fourteen separate hikes.

2. Hike each peak in every month of the year, as in summiting Old Speck in January, February, March, and so on, to December. This is termed the "grid" approach. Fourteen peaks summited twelve times each (for each month) totals 168 ascents! Completing the grid for Maine would ordinarily require years of hiking.

3. Reach the summit of every peak at night on a full moon.

4. Hike each of the forty-eight 4,000-Footers in New Hampshire in each of the four seasons ($48 \times 4 = 192$) and contribute forty-eight hours of volunteer work to the AMC.

There are yet more ways, described in the fine book *The 4000 Footers of the White Mountains* by Steven D. Smith and Mike Dickerman (see "Good Reads" at the end of this book). Perhaps you, reading this, might create one more new way!

Some hikers aim to move quickly. For the White Mountain 4,000-foot peaks, there are established speed records. I am not aware of such records for Maine. Others may wish to take their time; explore alpine flora, glacial erratic boulders, and tarns; do nature photography; or lie on their backs and watch the clouds fly overhead.

Certainly you may hike one or more of the fourteen peaks simply for the experience of doing so—without the goal of New England Four-Thousand-Footer Club recognition. Hundreds of hikers do so each year. The founding purpose of the FTFC was to encourage hikers to explore new territory. There is no one single way to hike Maine's 4,000-foot peaks.

Steve Smith and Mike Dickerman write of the original intent of the Four-Thousand-Footer Club, "*A hiker who climbs the 4000 footers comes away with a deeper appreciation of the mountain world, a knowledge he or she can share with other hikers starting out. That, in turn, may lead to a commitment to preserve and protect the fragile beauty of the mountains.*"

Hike your own hike!

Getting Ready

What to Wear and What to Carry

No matter the season, expect changeable weather on the high ground. The fall and winter wisdom of dressing in layers applies year-round.

I have encountered sleet on the Bigelow Range in late July, been battered by a chilling rain from an advancing cold front on North Crocker in August, and waded through shin-deep snow on Saddleback in early October when the sun was shining in the Sandy River Valley below.

Here is a sample list. Consult other sources. Take a course in hiking and backpacking. Make your own list!

- Hiking shoes. What is on your feet should provide good grip and stability. Maine trails can be muddy, even on dry days in summer. Blisters occur when footwear and feet are new to one another! Break in new shoes before hiking to high elevations—first on level to rolling ground, next on lower peaks, before committing to a high-peak trek.
- Layered clothing:
  - Wicking clothing next to skin, short or long sleeve.
  - Warm wicking layer such as a long-sleeve fleece.
  - Wind and rain shell, breathable.
  - Socks, wool or wicking synthetic material (pack a spare pair).
  - Shorts or hiking pants, quick drying.
  - Stocking cap and gloves or mittens; balaclava or neck gaiter for cold weather. These can also be handy on high ground and by lakeshores, even in summer.
- In the day pack:
  - Maps, both paper and electronic. See peak entries in this book for suggested maps.
  - Water sufficient for the hike up or out and the return. I carry a minimum of one liter, two liters for longer hikes and in warm weather. (Also leave water in your vehicle for all members of the hiking party at the end of the hike.) Carry a water-purification means (e.g., filter or chemical treatment) if the hike will be an extended one. Research water sources along the route.
  - Sustaining lunch/snack foods.
  - Small trash bag. Leave no trace, no wrappers, no orange peels—nothing, please.
  - Sun protection: sunscreen, lip balm, bandanna, sunglasses.
  - Insect repellent. Covering with clothing is advised. If you use repellent, keep it away from nylon and plastics and apply with the back of

the hand to avoid eye contact. Lotion is more efficient than spray—and keeps you and your companions from breathing spray.

- Biodegradable toilet paper and hand sanitizer.
- Notebook/sketchpad.
- Guides to wildflowers, birds, trees, mammals.
- Trekking poles or hiking staff. These are good for balance and saving wear and tear on the body and are especially useful for stream crossings and for steep step-downs.
- Water shoes or sandals to change into for wading in a stream pool or lake, where the bottom may be rock or mud.
- Towel (a small pack towel or an extra bandana or two may be all that is needed).

- A pack within the pack—the ready bag. I carry a small waterproof bag inside my day pack. It contains items that I may not need on most hikes, but when I need them, I really need them! These take up little room and do not weigh much. At some point in my hiking career, I have needed each item on the list!
    - Headlamp with fresh batteries and spare batteries—even if you don't expect to be out after dark.
    - Space blanket (reflective, heat-retaining blanket). These fold to the size of a wallet.
    - Compass (if contained within a battery-powered device, such as a phone or GPS unit, carry a separate compass in event of battery drain).
    - Fire starters: waterproof matches, lighter. I carry both.
    - First-aid supplies (think rolled ankle; scraped knee, elbow, or hand; blisters): adhesive bandages of different sizes, antiseptic, blister treatment, tape to wrap a rolled ankle.
    - Small knife.
    - Whistle (a default communication device if someone becomes separated from the party or has a mishap).
    - Spare warm socks. I have used these as mittens in suddenly cold weather, as water shoes to take a dip in a rocky stream, or as spare socks!
    - One or two bandanas (many uses).
    - Water-purification tablets.
    - Notebook/pencil.

The Ten Essentials

One approach to trip preparation is the concept of the Ten Essentials. Hiking parties review the categories and select particular items or make specific arrangements according to the terrain, season, weather, common mishaps, and demands of the itinerary.

The earliest Ten Essentials list appears to be that published by The Mountaineers, a Seattle-based outdoor club, in the book *Freedom of the Hills* in 1974.

Over the years the list has been modified in consideration of new developments of many kinds—from navigation tools to clothing to trail foods—as well as specific local terrain. Preparations for a desert hike will differ from those for a winter snow-shoe trek.

The underlying concept still holds: a party that carries items on the list, has the skills to use them properly, and engages in the recommended planning is likely to manage adverse conditions in the backcountry.

Compile Your Own List

Research a number of Ten Essentials lists. Consult with experienced hikers. Take an outdoor skills course. Discuss in your group what each person is carrying and how the group will function together.

A sample:

- Navigation, communication, signaling: Up-to-date maps showing contours and neighboring terrain; personal locator device, cell phone with spare power, distance whistle, fire starter material; bright-colored bandana; foil blanket (doubles as insulation—below).
- Illumination: Headlamp, spare batteries.
- Nutrition and hydration: Emergency food for overnight; sufficient water for hike up and hike down; water-purification means.
- Insulation: Rain, wind, and cold protection; spare base layer; watch cap, gloves or mitts, neck warmer, spare socks; insulating foil blanket.
- Protection: Sunscreen, lip screen, hat, sunglasses; first-aid supplies for mountain scenarios (hypothermia, hyperthermia, ankle or knee injury, large surface-area scrapes, finger cuts, blisters); repair kit for gear (rugged safety pins, repair tape).
- Sanitation: Supplies for toileting; instruction for the party on sanitary and safe practices; biodegradable materials; hand sanitizer.
- Preparation: Inform a responsible person of the itinerary, expected time of return, names and ages of others in the party, contact information for what authority to call in the event of an unexplained delay—which may be 911.
- Notification: Every member of the party should be informed of the itinerary; take more than one map per hiking party.
- Collaboration/cooperation: Hike as a group; agree on break intervals; do not divide a party into fast and slow subgroups.
- Anticipation: Set a turnaround time and stick to it; small notebook or note cards; pencil.

These items take up surprisingly little space and are of minimal weight.

LAYER UP

The old expression "mountains make their own weather" is certainly true for 4,000-foot peaks. Expect summit temperatures to be 5°F to 10°F colder than at the base of the mountain because temperatures typically drop 3°F to 5°F per 1,000 feet of elevation gain. That does not include the wind-chill effect from the winds that are fairly constant above the tree line.

I have encountered sleet on a July day, when there were off/on rain sprinkles in the valley, and a full-bore snowstorm during the first days of October, when the sun was shining on fall foliage by the highway below.

Pack layers: wool cap and gloves; a neck warmer; a warm, wicking layer; and a hooded rain/wind shell are standard gear in my day pack. If rain is in the forecast, I add rain pants to the list.

To be cold and wet on the ridgetop is to court hypothermia at worst and at best detracts from enjoying the accomplishment of bagging the summit. You work hard to get to the top! Enjoy it!

I advise all 4,000-Footer hikers to educate themselves about the Ten Essentials. Major retailers of quality outdoor gear and clothing provide such lists online, as do hiking clubs and organizations such as the Appalachian Mountain Club.

On the Trail

The Day of Your Hike

Start with ample time to return before dark: Early starts provide opportunities to see wildlife, to spend extra time in the area (if you wish), and to have plenty of time before dark if someone in the group is moving slowly or has a mishap. I prefer to be on trail at first light, typically by 6:00 a.m. At times of the year when sunrise is later, I may begin the hike by headlamp.

Inform every person in your party of the hiking plan: distance, weather report, expected difficult stretches of trail, anticipated time, turnaround time, and scheduled water and nutrition breaks. At a minimum, have two sets of navigation guides: maps, compasses, GPS. It is essential that more than one person (and preferably everyone in the party) have the information and skills to navigate in the backcountry.

Plan for breaks. Think of hiking as an athletic event for which the body needs sustaining nourishment and hydration. I stop about every ninety minutes for a five- to ten-minute water break and to eat something that will sustain me—such as an apple or banana, half a bagel, or nuts. These are usually standing breaks. Every three hours I will sit and put my feet up. Lunch is another one of these breaks, with a bit more food. The point is to maintain a sound nutritional level throughout the day. Avoid nutritional deficit.

Leave a written note with a responsible person. Describe where you are going, when you plan to return, and whom to contact if you do not show up as planned.

Confirm that each person has the necessary gear, food, water, clothing, and footwear. One person's unpreparedness can affect the entire hiking party.

DRINK AND EAT

How often to drink water on the trail? How often to eat? Hiking is demanding exercise. Avoid hydration or nutrition deficit, with the extra dimension of fatigue this condition brings. I take a standing water and food break every sixty to ninety minutes, depending upon ambient temperature and the extent of my effort.

I usually take two to three swigs and eat a small handful of nuts, or a piece of fruit, or part of a bagel or wrap with peanut butter, or half an energy bar (preferably a bar we have baked at home).

It is as vital to drink and eat on the descent, when a hiker is often fatigued, as it is on the ascent. I typically carry one to two liters of water and have a means of purification in case I run low. Water bottle mouthpiece filters, straw filters, pump filters, iodine tablets, and battery-operated devices are among the options.

Set aside water and food to be left in the vehicle for the return at the end of the hike. Your body needs replenishment. Eat. Drink water. You will still have an appetite when you get back to town or return home.

Hiking in a Group

For groups, even on a short hike, have a lead hiker and a sweeper hiker (at the end of the group). All other hikers walk between these two. No one runs on ahead. No one is left behind.

Keep together. In the event of an injury or illness, there may be no way to communicate with others if the group has divided.

Never leave someone behind to catch up later. A hiker who is moving slowly will travel more quickly in the supportive conversational company of others.

A slow, steady pace, even if quite slow, is less tiring than frequent starts and stops.

Turnaround Time

In every hiking season some hikers are caught out after dark unexpectedly. Setting a turnaround time reduces the chance that darkness will fall before a party returns.

Count the number of hours from the start time to sunset. Divide that number in half. Add this half to the start time. This is your turnaround time—the time to turn back, regardless of whether you have reached the mountaintop.

Example: You start a hike to Katahdin from Roaring Brook Campground at 6:00 a.m. on a day when sunset is at 7:00 p.m. That is a 13-hour time span; half of 13 is 6.5 hours. The turnaround time is 12:30 p.m. That leaves 6.5 hours until sunset.

On Katahdin and most 4,000-Footers, the time for descent may be equal to that for ascent. Fatigued hikers move slowly, particularly on the steep and rough trails common in this region. Low light, deteriorating weather, and slippery footpaths will contribute to slow going.

Be alert to the direction of the sunset! If your return hike is eastward, you will be hiking out in mountain shadow and have less remaining light.

Carry headlamps, with spare batteries, on every hike.

Dogs

I enjoy bringing our chocolate Labrador—leashed—on many hikes, but not all. Dogs, like people, do best on the trail when physically conditioned. Experience with the sights and sounds—and smells—of the mountains is vital.

Introduce your dog to hiking, to other hikers, and to other dogs on trail by practicing near home before taking a mountain hike.

Here are a few observations from a few decades with our own dogs and seeing others:

- Some terrain—mud, rock—will be difficult on your dog's feet. I have seen dogs just quit, lie down, and refuse to move on.

- With a dog in the woods, there is little chance that you will see wildlife. Ground-nesting birds such as ruffed grouse will be in extreme danger. Mammals, from squirrels to white-tailed deer, will opt for seclusion.
- Territoriality: You know about this from walks in your home neighborhood. On trail, whose territory is it when two (or more) dogs meet? Or the dog encounters new children and adults? Avoid putting your dog under territorial stress.
- Leashing: Admittedly, leashing is a sensitive subject for dog owners who consider their pet to be under voice control. Consider that a forest environment has many distractions (usually new scents) for a dog and that dog behavior in the Maine woods may be very different from that at home or in other familiar environments.
- I have encountered dogs that ran from their owners, chasing deer, and traveled miles from where their owners last saw them. At least twice in my experience the disappearance occurred on a Sunday afternoon hike, the dog could not be located by nightfall, and adults in the family had to report for work out of state the next day. What a quandary!
- Above tree line, dogs should be leashed. At high elevations birds and small mammals have their homes near ground level and have no protection for themselves and their young against a curious dog.
- I leash our dog to a chest harness instead of a collar to avoid neck injury on uneven ground.
- Clean up after your pet near water. Please.

Children

Children love to hike! Build success into your hikes. Keep the first few short, simple, and memorable. Walk to a spot with a distinguishing feature—a long view, a lakeside spot, or a waterfall.

Better to have a child say "I want to go on a longer hike next time" than "That hike was too long. I don't want to go hiking again."

Give children the opportunity to carry a pack, even if very light and containing something as simple as a jacket or snack. This is not a deal breaker, but they may enjoy carrying something. The best packs have a waist belt and do not flop around and become unwieldy. If buying a new pack is costly, check local thrift shops. (I have bought brand-name children's packs for a dollar!) Snug up the shoulder straps for comfort.

Sketch pads and journals work well with kids. Give them a chance to sit in the woods or at a viewing point and record what they see and hear. You may be amazed!

Wildlife, trees, and flowers are fascinating! Look at photo books before—and after—the hike.

Leave recorded music at home. For many families this is a hiking rule. Children will get used to it! Invite them to listen to the sounds of the forest.

Prepare for your upcoming hike by walking the same distance as the trail distance on level ground near home before hiking that same distance up a mountain and back.

Tell children how far you are going and how long it is expected to take. This can limit "are-we-there-yet's?"

Maintain scrapbooks of your hikes; include your child's sketches and perhaps a quote from a journal. Celebrate that time in the outdoors! But avoid photo shoots and selfies as a substitute for looking! Children will gain more from drawing what they see than from snapping photos.

Water

All backcountry water should be treated before drinking. Water that looks clear is not necessarily safe to drink. Treatments include water filters, water purification tablets, and boiling.

Sanitation

When toileting, please step off the trail. Dig a hole in the ground with a hiker's trowel, a rock, or your boot. Deposit biodegradable toilet paper in the hole and cover. Please do not litter the forest with toilet paper.

Navigation

The distances provided in this book are derived from a variety of authorities, including published maps, publications of trail-maintaining organizations, and signage. In turn, a variety of measurement methods have been used by such sources. Hikers will find differences among various sources and often when in the field will come upon signage that differs from published data. I have even seen two signs only a few feet apart on the same trail with different mileage figures!

Measurements over the years have been made by hiking pace, measuring wheel rolled along a trail, determining distance off a map rather than on the ground, surveying equipment, GPS, and, most recently, light detection and ranging (LiDAR). There is a time lag between determinations made using the latest measurement technology and the entry of that information on a map, in a book, or on a trail sign.

Expect differences. These are ordinarily not significant. In time the signage will change—although another new technology will come along!

Choosing Maps

I commonly use a combination of maps, rather than one single map, to have the benefit of different features and information.

- United States Geological Survey (USGS) topographic maps: Excellent to identify features in the field and for compass navigation; valuable for reading the terrain. For emergency purposes, I always carry a contour map. Newer trails and recent trail relocations may not be depicted on USGS maps.

- Local trail map: In this book, recent maps published by Baxter State Park, the Maine Bureau of Parks and Lands, and the Maine Appalachian Trail Club. Detailed maps designed for hiker use, depicting distance, elevation gain, contours, water sources, side trails, and campsites.
- Regional map: I use the *DeLorme Maine Atlas & Gazetteer*, 2019 edition, a resource useful for locating trailheads, particularly in remote areas; it provides a broad view of the surrounding region, including nearby peaks, towns, state parks, camping facilities, and mountain roads. Newer trails and trail routes may not be depicted on DeLorme maps. Not intended for on-trail navigation.

GPS

While GPS devices have become quite common among hikers, outdoors people have traveled quite well for centuries (millennia) without them. I have GPS devices but always carry a paper map on my hikes. Why so? It is a good practice to see features of the terrain around me and to anticipate the terrain to come. Paper maps help me to do that. I can look out from a viewing point, see a ridge or a stream valley, and place myself on the map.

Online Apps and Maps

A sizable and growing number of online resources are available for backcountry navigation. I use them but do not recommend any one such resource here. Rather, I encourage you to consult with experienced users, including staff at well-regarded outfitters, Maine Guides, or instructors of local courses in such navigation.

My standards call for contour lines and side trails, a downloadable map, and confidence that the underlying map source is current. Trail reroutings are common. Also, trail closures may occur because of late snow cover, weather damage, owner use on private lands, and timber harvests—making it vital to have a view of surrounding terrain and prospective alternate routes.

I always carry paper maps, and I inquire locally about current conditions before setting out on a hike.

North, South, East, West in This Book

You will find in this book two sets of terms for directions:

- Direction of the Appalachian Trail (AT): AT North or AT South. Maps and signage for the AT use north and south to refer to the direction of the trail as it leads to its northern terminus, Katahdin in Maine, or to its southern terminus, Springer Mountain in Georgia. There is no AT East or AT West because the AT is a north–south trail. The compass direction of AT North at any given point could be north, east, west, or even south. If the particular direction leads eventually to Katahdin, the trail is AT North. The same terminology applies to AT South. Example: At the junction of the Sugarloaf Mountain spur trail with the AT, take the AT North to reach Caribou Pond Road—even though Caribou Pond Road is (compass) west of the Sugarloaf Trail. The trail in that direction leads eventually to Katahdin.

- North, south, east, or west otherwise: When not referring to the direction of the AT, I use the conventional meaning of north, south, east, and west (i.e., the general compass direction).

Lost?

Becoming lost on the short trails described in this book is rare. Keep your party together. Never leave slower hikers behind to catch up later.

When stepping off the trail for toileting, mark the trail with a trekking pole and bright bandana. Do not enter the woods beyond the distance you can see the pole.

If you are lost, stop walking. Sit down. Gather your wits. Use what methods you know to calm yourself. You are likely closer to the trail now than you might be if you rush off in a random direction.

- Attempt to contact your party by cell phone. Text may work where a voice call does not.

- Attempt to contact 911. Locate your vicinity on your map. Give your location as best you can, noting landmarks you can see or recently passed.

- Conserve battery power.

- Each person in the Maine woods should carry a quality whistle. Whistles may be heard at a far greater distance than the human voice. Signal with the whistle with a series of three blasts—standard signal of an emergency.

- Help yourself to be found—make yourself visible. Get into an open area, marking your path from the location where you start. Build a safe fire. Maintain it as a signal, night and day. A fire is one of the most effective means of signaling your location. Continue to use the whistle.

- Keep warm and dry using the extra clothing you have packed and a wind-blocking, warmth-retaining layer such as a foil blanket. In wet conditions, place a barrier between yourself and the ground.

- Eat from your spare food. Keep hydrated.

- Gather dry firewood to maintain your fire and for exercise and morale.

- If you have a personal locator device, activate it.

- If you step away from your open area, such as to look for water, mark your trail in a very visible way so you can find your way back to the open site.

Cell Phones

Kindly understand that many hikers seek out the forests, mountaintops, and wild waters in order to enjoy the sounds of the wind and the birds—and even the sound of silence. Think concert hall or house of worship.

As a courtesy to other hikers, keep your phone turned off or in airplane or reduced-battery-load mode. This is also a good move to conserve battery power for a true emergency.

If you must make a call, please move to an area well beyond earshot of other hikers.

In many of the remote areas in this book, there may be no reliable cell phone service. Using airplane or reduced-battery-load mode will prevent the phone from using up battery life searching for a signal.

Care for your phone as an emergency device.

Guide to the Entries

- Peak name and mountain range: Alternate names provided where applicable.
- Location: Town or township; park, preserve, or other public land; private land.
- Elevation: Source data from the Four-Thousand-Footer Club of the Appalachian Mountain Club (2019).
- Rank: 1–14, with 1 as highest.
- Elevation gain: Approximate difference between trailhead and summit elevations. Figure may be modified upward if there is an elevation loss and gain on the route, adding to net gain.
- Lands traversed: Public land unit, such as parkland; privately held land.
- Nearby supply town: Lodging, food, hiking gear, and/or vehicle services. (See appendices for town-by-town resources.)
- Fee: Yes/no; description.
- Maps: USGS topographic map(s); local trail maps delineating the trail; DeLorme Maine Atlas regional maps for trailhead access.
- Features: Origin of name; historical events; views; topography, including rivers, streams, lakes, nearby peaks, rock outcrops, glacial cirques, and the like.
- Single-peak itineraries: Day-hike route to this one 4,000-foot peak only.
- Multiple-peak itineraries: Day hike to the *peak of focus and one or more neighboring 4,000-foot peaks.* (See "Backpacking Maine's 4,000-Footers" in the "Out of the Ordinary" section of this book for sample overnight itineraries.)
- Approach trail(s): Trailhead, trail markings, trail-maintaining organization. For each entry: name of trail; trailhead driving directions; trailhead amenities (e.g., trailhead sign, parking area, information kiosk, privy); trail markings—color of blazes; maintaining entity; distance to summit.
- On trail: Observations from one or more hikes I have taken on each trail.
- Bird's-eye map: Overview of trail route and surrounding territory. Not intended for on-trail navigation.

Peaks and Trails

Mahoosuc Range

The Mahoosucs reach north and east of Gorham and Shelburne, New Hampshire, to Grafton Notch in Maine. Wild, rugged terrain includes the notorious Mahoosuc Notch, dubbed the hardest mile on the Appalachian Trail (AT), with its jumble of boulders for hikers to crawl over and even under. Fine views stretch to the Presidential Range and the Carter-Moriah Range and to the less frequently visited mountain country lying northward toward Canada. Old Speck is the highest peak in the range and commands a striking view southward over a dozen or more peaks from the watchtower on its summit.

Old Speck Mountain

Range: Mahoosuc
Location: Grafton Township
Elevation: 4,170 feet
Rank: 5
Elevation gain: 2,700 feet
Lands traversed: Grafton Notch State Park; Appalachian Trail Corridor
Fee: State park seasonal day use fee; self-pay station at Highway 26 parking lot

Nearby supply town: Bethel, 16 miles
Maps: USGS Old Speck Mountain; Grafton Notch State Park and Mahoosuc Public Lands Map, State of Maine (https://maine.gov); MATC AT Strip Map #7, Maine Highway 17 to New Hampshire state line; DeLorme Maine Atlas Map #18, 1-E

The speckled appearance of high gray ledge and deep green spruce-fir growth on steeply rising slopes gives Old Speck its name. This former fire-tower peak caps the northern end of the rugged Mahoosuc Range, looming over Grafton Notch and the swift-running Bear River. Hikers may enjoy 360-degree views from the summit observation platform, reached by a 30-foot steel ladder.

Sharply cut Grafton Notch and the sub-4,000-foot Baldpate Range lie north of the summit. The distinctive Saddleback Range, with two 4,000-Footers, rises beyond to the northeast. The Mahoosuc Range itself stretches southwesterly toward the Carter-Moriah Range and the Presidential Range—including Mt. Washington—in New Hampshire. Nearer in that direction are Speck Pond (highest fishable body of water in Maine), the rounded peak of curiously named Mahoosuc Arm, and the upper reach of notorious Mahoosuc Notch—termed the most difficult mile on the entire 2,190-mile AT.

Old Speck is the southernmost 4,000-foot peak in Maine, 33.5 trail miles north of New Hampshire's 4,049-foot Mt. Moriah and 46.3 miles south of 4,120-foot Saddleback.

Start anywhere on the 4,000-Footer list, but Old Speck certainly offers a good introduction to Maine high-peak hiking: steadily ascending, rocky trail; snow lingering into spring and arriving early in fall; subalpine spruce-fir forest at higher elevations; miniature falls on clear Cascade Brook; cliff-edge views along the upper edge of the Notch; thick trailside carpets of rock moss and sphagnum; appropriate underfoot amounts of mud and roots to talk about when the hike is done; long views.

I hike Old Speck about once per year. Having cut my teeth on New Hampshire's 4,000-Footers in my youth, I enjoy the twin sets of views—south toward the White Mountains of my New Hampshire roots, north to the Maine mountains that have been my home for much of my adult life. The usually modest waterfalls on Cascade Brook transform at spring or after a hard rain to roar down a channel carved over millennia. Mosses in the sheltered trail section midway to the summit are magical, amassing a foot thick around the base of the balsam fir.

- Single-peak itinerary: Old Speck by the AT South from Grafton Notch.
- Multiple-peak itineraries: None—Old Speck is the only 4,000-foot peak in the region.
- Approach trails: AT (Old Speck) and Mahoosuc Range Trail.
- Trailhead: Grafton Notch State Park parking areas, Maine Highway 26, 9.5 miles north of junction with US Route 2. Parking, self-pay station, vault toilets, information kiosk, hiker register.
- Markers: Old Speck Trail, white blazes (AMC); Eyebrow Trail, orange blazes (AMC); Mahoosuc Range Trail, spur to summit, blue blazes (AMC).
- Maintainer: AMC.
- Distance to summit: 3.8 miles one way (OW); 7.6 miles round-trip (RT) (Eyebrow Trail adds 0.1 mile to the OW; not advised for descent).
- Points of interest:
      Grafton Notch State Park parking area/trailhead.
      0.1 Eyebrow Trail, lower junction.
      0.9 Cascade stream.
      1.0 Eyebrow Trail, upper junction.
      3.0 Viewing point over Grafton Notch.
      3.5 Mahoosuc Range Trail junction, spur trail to summit.
      3.8 Old Speck summit: 4,170 feet.

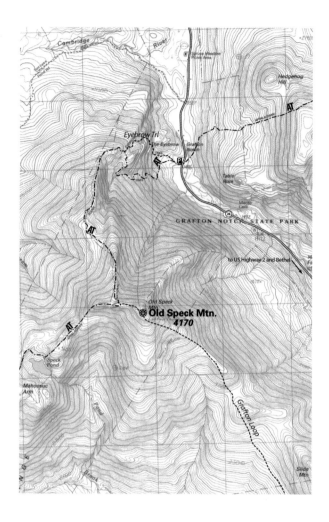

AT South

One of my recent ascents of Old Speck is on a mild October day, as overnight rain ceases and the sky brightens. I sign in at the trail kiosk at the north side of the Highway 26 parking area—no other vehicles but mine at 7:00 a.m.—and head out. In 0.1 mile the Eyebrow Trail diverges diagonally to the right. This steep trail rejoins the Old Speck Trail in 1.1 miles after ascending to the ledges above Eyebrow Cliff.

The Old Speck Trail swings left, passes by stands of American beech, bears more easterly, and steadily ascends rock steps through hardwoods and a smattering of balsam fir. As I gain elevation, I pass sluice runs and falls on Cascade Brook, roaring in full freshness. The trail ascends toward the north–south rolling ridge, which it will follow over much of the way to the summit. Over my left shoulder the sun breaks through the cloud cover to brighten late-season trickles of falling water on Cascade Brook. The trail turns south, climbs steadily, passes two lookout points with views above to the distant, looming summit and into Grafton Notch below. At one hour of hiking on trail, I pass the Eyebrow Trail junction, which enters on the right.

My route swings left, as the Old Speck Trail proceeds over a series of knolls, steadily gaining elevation, moving in a great arc from Eyebrow Cliff to the peak. A ground ladder holds the slope in one spot. I am well into the conifers at this elevation, where hemlock, spruce, and fir predominate. Views open in the slowly dissipating morning mist down into the Notch and toward the valley of the Swift River. Across Grafton Notch, West Baldpate, East Baldpate hidden behind it, rises above lingering clouds. It is a rare view—the summit jutting out of surrounding cloud cover, morning sun hitting the exposed peaks. Quite the sight!

Mosses cover much of the trailside ground and even grow up and around the base of the firs. This section of trail is well shaded for much of the year—offering ideal moisture and cover for moss to thrive. The ups and downs continue, with an occasional scramble or pitch climb where the trail has worn down to ledge. A half mile before the ridgetop intersection with the Mahoosuc Trail are more northward lookout points.

Shortly after a seep on the left, where water drips from overhanging moss, the trail makes a final steady ascent to meet the Mahoosuc Trail, which enters right.

The Old Speck Trail ends here, but the white blazes continue south as the Mahoosuc Trail becomes the AT South. Speck Pond, Mahoosuc Arm, Mahoosuc Notch, and, eventually, New Hampshire lie in that direction.

Speck Pond is a magnificent high-elevation pond, with a lean-to and tent sites (fee) managed by the Appalachian Mountain Club (AMC). The caretaker is on-site during the summer season. I have camped here and enjoyed a bracing dip in the clear, sharply cold water. However, be advised that the descent to the pond (and return for those contemplating a round-trip hike) is quite steep, dropping down over exposed ledge. Expect four-point scrambling. This route makes for slow going in wet weather. I would allow a minimum of two hours for the round trip, not counting time spent at the pond.

One fall morning I take the weather forecasters at their word and pull into the Grafton Notch trailhead parking area just as an overnight rain ceases. Low clouds lie over the Notch as I head up the trail.

As I gain elevation, I pass the falls on Cascade Brook, roaring in fresh fullness, and ascend toward a series of high knobs between the brook and the summit, never far from drop-offs along the edge of the Notch. Short herd paths lead 20 to 30 feet to lookout points.

The Notch is covered in woolly white. The peaks of the Baldpate Range across the Notch and Old Speck above poke through the cloud cover and shine in the light of bright morning sun. Quite the sight.

Back on trail at the summit ridge, I turn a sharp left on the blue-blazed Mahoosuc Trail to ascend the final 0.3 mile to the summit tower and a small clearing. The former fire-tower cab has been removed. The tower has been rebuilt, with a small observation platform, reached by ascending a 30-foot steel ladder. The rungs are slippery in wet weather, and ascending is not advised in such conditions. Today, however, has become dry and clear—a fine day for this 360-degree view.

The great mass of the White Mountains rises to the southwest. To the north lie the peaks of Coos County in New Hampshire, the sub-4,000-foot mountains that border Quebec, and prominent Maine peaks of Aziscohos and West Kennebago. Against the northeast skyline stands the jumble of Maine 4,000-Footers that cluster in Franklin and Somerset Counties. The pond to the immediate west and below is Speck Pond, blue among surrounding dark conifers. Beyond the pond, the cliffs of curiously named Mahoosuc Arm fall away to the sharp fold of Mahoosuc Notch, its mile-long boulder-strewn floor hidden from this vantage point.

Mahoosuc Notch is described as the most difficult mile on the AT. I have clambered through it many times—over boulders, letting myself down others, even crawling under blocks that have tumbled from the Notch walls to rest on other boulders, creating short squeeze routes with a hint—but only a hint—of spelunking. My Mahoosuc Notch time usually comes in at around two hours—for that one mile! Tough as that trail section is, many hikers will say—as I do—that the steep climb from the south up Mahoosuc Arm is pretty tough in its own right.

I descend the tower to enjoy some lunch—and attract two gray jays (a.k.a. camp robbers). These quite un-shy birds like to hang around canoe trip campsites. I had not expected them up here. But they know what they are doing. I have macaroni, cheese, and tomato—hearty for the work I am doing this day—which I cooked at the last minute before I left home and is still warm. When I spill some, the jays cock their heads and flit close, waiting for me to depart.

Time to go. A pair of hikers arrives just as I am leaving. They are from Bethel on a day hike. In moments I meet southbound AT hiker Pat. He left Katahdin in early October and plans to hike to Gorham and resume his AT hike in the next season. That is wise. The Presidential Range is already draped in snow. When Emma Gatewood summited Old Speck on her historic 1955 hike of the entire AT, she reported freezing rain and sleet up here—on September 3!

On the descent I take time to step to each viewing point, to have another look at the beds of thick moss, and to take a break by Cascade Brook before I reach the trailhead.

Nearby Hikes
Eyebrow Trail Loop

The Eyebrow Trail is a 1.1-mile route that begins at mile 0.1 on the Old Speck Trail. It gains 1,030 feet in elevation in that distance before rejoining the Old Speck Trail. The route crosses fairly level to moderately rising terrain at first before climbing steeply through the trees to the right of Eyebrow Cliff. Once you are on the ledges above the cliff, the ascent part of the hike is essentially over, and the route moves near-laterally to a junction with Old Speck Trail. Views from the top of the cliff are exceptional—to the Old Speck summit and down into Grafton Notch.

The most challenging section of the Eyebrow Trail is the crossing of a sharply sloped drainage, where water runs down over open ledge and slick moss creates slippery conditions. As hiker aids, trail builders have installed a cable bolted to the trailside ledge, a series of iron rungs placed laterally across the rock face, and a 5-foot metal ladder at the short pitch at the end of the traverse.

Given the focused attention that must be given to foot placement and balance in this section, the Eyebrow Trail is not advisable for children, for dogs, and for those uncomfortable with exposure to steep trail. This route is not advised for descent. Hikers usually descend to the parking area by way of the Old Speck Trail.

I have hiked Old Speck by including the Eyebrow Trail in the ascent. It is well worth the effort and added ten minutes or so to my total hiking time to reach the summit. However, I have encountered a party that brought a dog on this trail against advice, but the dog, perhaps wanting nothing to do with rungs and a ladder, ran off.

Enjoy this route. Exercise caution.

Speck Pond by Mahoosuc Range Trail (AT)

The Mahoosuc Range Trail continues 1.1 miles southwest from the Old Speck summit to the AMC campsite at 9-acre Speck Pond (lean-to and tent sites). This route is in the Mahoosuc Public Lands Unit and also within the Appalachian Trail Corridor.

The pond is at the highest elevation of any pond in Maine and is open to fishing (see "Out of the Ordinary: Fishing the 4,000-Footers," later in this book). It is stocked with brook trout by the Maine Department of Inland Fisheries and Wildlife. A Maine fishing license is required.

The route offers fine views over the Mahoosuc Range and toward Mahoosuc Arm and the fold of Mahoosuc Notch as it descends steep ledge shortly after leaving the junction with the Old Speck Trail. Hikers will want to keep their eyes on their feet as well, as the trail loses nearly 500 feet of elevation in the first 0.4 mile. Expect four-point hiking (hands and feet) in this section, which is difficult when the ledge is wet.

The trail moderates near its halfway point and is nearly level for a short stretch before resuming steady descent in the final 0.4 mile to the campsite.

For those on a day hike, a round-trip hike from Old Speck to Speck Pond could require up to two hours (more in slippery conditions). That does not include time spent at the pond itself, presumably one to two additional hours, for a total of four hours to be added to the return hike to the trailhead at Grafton Notch.

To enjoy Speck Pond to the fullest, without the time crunch of a day hike, consider a backpacking trip, such as the full Mahoosuc Range from Shelburne, New Hampshire, to Grafton Notch.

There is an AMC caretaker on-site at the pond. A fee is charged for overnight use. In 2019, that fee was $10 per person per night (no fee for day hikers). Camping groups larger than five persons should contact the AMC (go to https://www.out doors.org or call 603-466-2721, ext. 8150) at least two weeks ahead of time to discuss proposed date(s) of use and obtain information on conditions of use.

Grafton Loop Trail (West)

The Grafton Loop Trail is one of the newer distance trails in the Maine mountains, constructed between 2006 and 2008 through cooperative efforts of the Maine Bureau of Parks and Land, the Maine Appalachian Trail Club (MATC), the Appalachian Mountain Club, and thoughtful private landowners. The trailhead for both East and West sections is on the east side of Highway 26, 4.9 miles north of US Route 2.

The west section ascends Old Speck, meeting the Mahoosuc Trail at the summit. The 13.3-mile distance from trailhead to summit (26.6 miles RT) or 17.1 miles OW from the loop trail west parking to the Highway 26 Old Speck parking area in the state park are impractical for a day hike. For backpackers there are four tent sites along the way. On route the trail ascends to the open summit of 3,335-foot Sunday River Whitecap. Here there are one-of-a-kind striking views of Old Speck to the north, the Baldpate Range to the northeast, the Mahoosuc Range to the northwest, and the Carter-Moriah and Presidential Ranges in the far west.

See "Backpacking Maine's 4,000-Footers" in the "Out of the Ordinary" section of this book.

Saddleback Range

Glacial striations, great erratic boulders, wild-appearing flag trees, alpine flowers—diapensia and such—deer sedge, high mountain tarns, long views over the Rangeley Lakes Chain and the sweep of the Sandy River Valley—welcome to the Saddleback Range! This is one of my favorite places. I ascend to the high ground year-round and in a full range of its weather moods (with proper gear, of course): clear, see-forever days, blowing rain, piling-up snow. The new (2016) Berry Picker's Trail (BPT) and the base-arcing Fly Rod Crosby Trail (FRCT) create many options for approaching Saddleback and reaching its heights.

The full length of the Range is 13.5 miles from the Sandy River in the southwest to Orbeton Canyon in the northeast. Saddleback has the longest stretch of above-tree-line trail in Maine, outside the Katahdin Tableland.

Saddleback Mountain

Range: Saddleback Range (a.k.a. Rangeley Mountains)
Location: Sandy River Plantation
Elevation: 4,120 feet
Rank: 8
Elevation gain: Varies by trailhead; up to 2,500 feet
Land units traversed: Appalachian Trail Corridor; Maine Appalachian Trail Land Trust, Orbeton Stream Conservation Easement; private lands—depending upon chosen trail

Nearby supply town: Rangeley
Fee: None
Maps: USGS Saddleback Mountain; MATC AT Strip Map #5, Maine Highway 27 to Maine Highway 17; DeLorme Maine Atlas Map #28, 5-E; 29, 1-E, 2-E. A Fly Rod Crosby Trail map may be useful to access Berry Picker's Trail and other Saddleback-area footpaths.

You can see in every direction from Saddleback, a former fire-tower peak: north to Quebec; south to the Camden Hills along Penobscot Bay; west to the Presidential Range; and northeast to Katahdin. In between lies the expanse of the Rangeley Lakes, the wild mountain border country to the north with many a trailless peak, and the irregular cant of eight other 4,000-foot peaks immediately to the northeast. To the south runs the broad expanse of the Sandy River Valley, gathering and channeling mountain runoff on its way to the 50-mile-distant Kennebec River, and from there to the Gulf of Maine at Merrymeeting Bay.

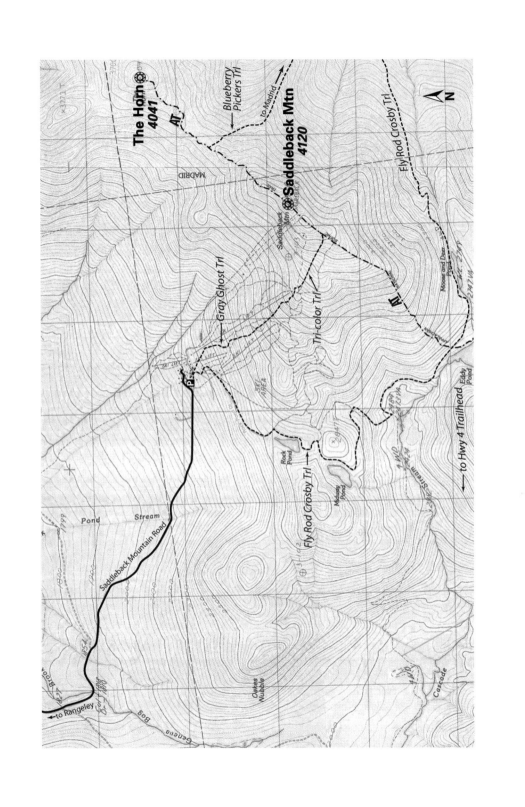

- Single-peak itineraries: AT North from Highway 4 trailhead; Berry Picker's Trail via Fly Rod Crosby Trail (south slope); Saddleback ski area alpine trails: Gray Ghost and Tri-Color.
- Multiple-peak itineraries: Many hikers combine a hike of Saddleback and The Horn.
- Approach trails: Saddleback Range Trail/AT; Berry Picker's Trail; Saddleback ski area alpine and hiking trail; Fly Rod Crosby Trail.
- Trail: Saddleback Range Trail/AT, Maine Highway 4, west side of highway, 9 miles southeast of Rangeley. Sign, parking area; no facilities.
- Markers: White blazes; MATC maintained.
- Distance to summit: 5.7 miles (11.4 miles RT).
- Points of interest:
    Highway 4 AT parking area. Trailhead (AT North) is across the highway.
    0.1 Sandy River footbridge.
    0.7 Beech Hill Road (gravel).
    1.5 Stream.
    1.8 Piazza Rock lean-to/campsite.
    (Blue-blazed side trail leads 0.1 mile to Piazza Rock outcrop and Piazza Rock Caves.)
    2.6 Ethel Pond, west shore.
    3.6 Eddy Pond (viewable to left [west] through trees 100 yards).
    3.7 Fly Rod Crosby Trail (gravel, multiuse).
    4.7 Tree line.
    5.5 First knob, trail junction (sign) for Saddleback Ski Area hiking route.
    5.7 Saddleback summit: 4,120 feet.

Saddleback Range Trail/AT North

The Sandy River route to Saddleback is one of the more magnificent approach trails in eastern North America. In a moment or two after passing the trailhead sign, I reach the Sandy River, here a quick-running narrow mountain stream, slicing through the gap formed by hand-set stone cribwork, to cross by a six-foot bridge. This first section of the trail was once an old road that wound up the Sandy River Valley, an effort to form a more direct route to Rangeley from points south than the roundabout way through Orbeton Canyon, past Redington Pond, and on into Rangeley from the northeast. The stonework has outlasted much newer bridges downstream, which collapsed or were spun over in the great flood of 1987.

I pause to inspect the work and imagine the crews here decades ago, building that road. The trail swings left (northwest) to ascend a set of steps out of the stream cut and turns right (northeast). I ascend gradually on fairly level ground, in a transition zone of mixed hardwood-softwood forest, rock maples, and yellow birch mixed in with spruce and fir.

Between the river and Piazza Rock campsite, I cross the old Beech Hill Road, a gravel road that once connected Madrid Village to foothills west of Saddleback.

A lookout point to the right of the trail (south) provides a long view over the Sandy River Valley. I pass through a close, well-shaded fir corridor, cross a series of bog bridges, reach a stream at 1.5 miles, and arrive at Piazza Rock. This is a popular day-hike destination for families and also a frequent overnight stop for backpackers on the way to the Crocker Range and Highway 27 and for AT through-hikers. Piazza Rock is worth seeing—a great porch to some, like the bow of a ship to others—jutting out of the mountainside. The nearby caves are worth a look—not true caverns but rock slabs and great boulders juxtaposed.

The campsite privy is a curiosity. It is a two-holer, curious enough. But between the two stations is a cribbage board, a permanent fixture of the privy. I have yet to come upon an active cribbage game here, but this is not a rainy day. People are hiking, not playing cards.

Beyond Piazza Rock, the number of people on trail drops, the angle of ascent rises, and the footpath is rockier. Pristine Ethel Pond lies on the right at 0.8 mile, glacier formed, like its neighbor, Eddy Pond, 1.0 mile farther. Those who combine fly-fishing with peak-bagging might want to allow time for one or both of these. The trail does not pass the shore of Eddy Pond. Look to the left twenty to thirty minutes beyond Ethel Pond. To protect the fragile shoreline growth, the former Maine Forest Service campsite by the pond has been discontinued. Beyond Eddy Pond, I reach the multiuse Fly Rod Crosby Trail, a gravel road where in summer hikers share the route with those on ATVs; in winter, those on cross-country skis or snowshoes share the route with snowmobilers. I come here often in winter—to snowshoe to the pond or as part of a long ski from the north side of Saddleback to Madrid to the south.

Time to go to work. The AT crosses the Crosby Trail to begin a steady ascent over the final 2.0 miles to the summit. Softwoods predominate here, with an occasional white birch.

There are some long reaches. A set of iron rungs form a ladder to ascend a 12-foot rock slab. The firs thin, and I reach the tree line, officially where the trees rise no higher than 5 feet. I am soon beyond any that approach that height and reach open ledge, where views begin to open up to the south. Cairns supplement white blazes to mark the way.

I pass many an erratic boulder and step over glacial striations. This is krummholz territory, where stunted and twisted fir and birch lie in great, twisted formations, low to the ground. A northwest wind blows. I move upward to a junction with an old footpath that connects with alpine ski trails on the north slope of the mountain at 5.5 miles.

A new trail sign, lodged in a cairn, was installed at this location in 2020, to replace the former sign, blown away in a high wind over a decade ago.

This is a significant junction. The north-direction trail descends as a rocky woods route 0.1 mile to the top of the broad Tri-Color ski trail of the Saddleback Mountain ski area. From there it is an additional 1.7 miles to the base lodge and the Saddleback Mountain Road. If a party needed to descend from the ridge for emergency purposes, this is the shortest route.

This is a rare alpine zone! Look for diapensia, mountain azalea, and mountain cranberry. The footpath is marked by stones to avoid hiker traffic on delicate alpine soil and fragile plants. I stick to the trail.

The Saddleback summit is 0.2 mile on the AT beyond the first knob and signpost, visible with a summit sign. The trail descends into a slight col before reaching this open summit and 360-degree view. Katahdin rests on the far northeastern skyline; Mt. Washington is to the southwest; coastal peaks of the Camden Hills and Cadillac Mountain in Acadia National Park line the southeast horizon; northward, the northern peaks of Franklin County and the border peaks with Quebec complete the picture.

Other hikers have constructed a low rock windbreak to the southeast of the summit, near a stand of fir that enjoys just enough protection from the angle of the summit to gain relief from prevailing northwest winds.

The Horn, the neighboring 4,000-Footer, rises 1.6 miles beyond on the AT.

Even if your destination for the day has been Saddleback itself, a short hike of 0.2 mile farther in the direction of The Horn will bring you to another knob and a striking view of that high peak and the long Saddleback col that gives the range its name. I make my way to this spot on many a Saddleback hike, taking my ridgetop break here.

Reverse direction for the return hike to the Highway 4 trailhead. For details on a hike to The Horn, see the next chapter.

Nearby Trails
Berry Picker's Trail

From the Highway 4–Reeds Mill Road junction in Madrid, Maine, drive east (one-lane bridge) on paved Reeds Mill Road for 3.0 miles. Cross a bridge over Conant Stream, where a house on the right immediately before the bridge is #639, and immediately at the end of the bridge, on the left, is a sign on a tree marking #640. Turn left on the narrow, dirt and gravel (and, in spring and summer, impassably muddy) so-called Epstein Road (no sign). Look on the right for a house, #642.

If the Epstein Road is blocked or is impassable because of weather conditions, do not proceed, and do not park here. Instead, approach Saddleback Range from one of the other routes in this book. This is private property. Kindly respect landowners. I have used this road many times without incident, but some would-be hikers have attempted to drive here when the road was washed out or too muddy and become stuck. Others have parked here without permission.

Once on the Epstein Road drive north 3.2 miles to a Y-intersection with snow-mobile trail ITS (Interconnected Trail System) 84/89, marked by yellow signs. Bear left (west). Cross a bridge rebuilt in the summer of 2019. Park in the open area just beyond the bridge, at mile 3.3. Here the Epstein Road proceeds straight (west). On-foot access to the Berry Picker's Trail continues via ITS 84/89 northward past the metal frame for a red gate. No motor vehicle access is permitted beyond this point.

The Berry Picker's Trail trailhead is 1.4 miles north from this parking spot. Approximately 0.9 mile from parking area reach the Fly Road Crosby Trail (FRCT) junction. Continue left (west) on ITS and FRCT to reach Berry Picker's Trail at Winship Stream (prominent sign).

- Markers: Snowmobile and Appalachian Trail Conservancy signs beyond Y-intersection; Fly Rod Crosby Trail signs and blue blazes; blue blazes beyond on Berry Picker's Trail.
- Maintainer: BPT: MATC maintained; Fly Rod Crosby section: diamond trail markers, FRCT maintained.
- Distance to Saddleback summit: 1.4-mile snowmobile trail walk + 1.7 miles BPT + 0.8 mile AT South = 3.9 miles (7.8 miles RT).
- Points of interest:
    Reed's Mill Road at Conant Stream: 3.3-mile drive to Y-intersection, left to planked Conant Stream bridge and parking area. Walk 1.4 miles north on ITS 84/89 to Berry Picker's Trail trailhead at Winship Stream (sign).
    0.2 Last access to Winship Stream (last water).
    0.9 Boundary ledges.
    1.3 Glacial erratic boulder.
    1.7 AT junction. Hike AT South.
    2.5 Saddleback summit: 4,120 feet.

The Berry Picker's Trail, opened in October 2016, provides the first maintained southern access to the Saddleback Range. Much of the route follows that of a local trail used to reach wild blueberry bushes growing high on this slope. When the AT was in the planning stage, it was considered as a route to connect Saddleback and Mt. Abraham but was not chosen in order to include The Horn and points now AT North on the route. I like the varied landscape—quick-running Winship Stream, open ledges, great boulders, distinct views toward Mt. Abraham Range and upward toward The Horn and Saddleback Junior.

The hike is a shorter alternative to the Highway 4–AT North route and has wilder surroundings than the Saddleback alpine ski trail route. It also makes possible an ascent of The Horn without climbing Saddleback first, if that is a consideration.

I find the driving directions quick to master. On my first trip, I stop to introduce myself to residents standing by the turn from Reeds Mill Road. They appreciate my stop, confirm directions for me, tell me of some unfortunate experiences with would-be hikers, and welcome me to continue to the trailhead.

BPT is well cut, well blazed, and straightforward to follow. On my latest hike, a companion and I hiked with Winship Stream to our left for 0.2 mile before the trail angles right. This is the last water source but also a spot to keep in mind for cooling off on the return hike. Two pools invite a dip, or at least a good splash. Don't expect to swim here.

Mixed hardwood-softwood soon transitions to balsam fir predominance. Bunchberry and bluebead lily flower trailside in good numbers. We reach so-called boundary ledge, where yellow paint blazes divide former private property owners. The BPT switches back and forth across sections of ledge to take advantage of open space. I watch the blue paint blazes carefully, as the route is not obvious in places. Views from the ledges over the Sandy River Valley are exceptional: Mt. Blue (iconic peak of southern Franklin County) and the Tumbledown-Jackson Range loom to the west.

A great boulder lies on one section of open ledge, about the size of a small elephant! This same boulder may be clearly seen from above at an outcrop in the saddle leading to The Horn. The trail moves away from the ledge to gain elevation through thick firs, en route to the AT in the saddle, 0.8 mile AT North from Saddleback and 0.8 mile AT South of The Horn. The junction is well signed.

To reach Saddleback, we turn left to ascend steeply, emerging quickly from the shelter of balsam fir, to make our way to the high ground. Long reaches require some four-point hiking, as we scramble up steep pitches. At a point 0.6 mile from the BPT, we reach a knob with a dramatic view of The Horn and a good look at the main peak of Saddleback, with its summit sign.

Reverse direction to return to the trailhead at the base of the mountain or to hike AT North to The Horn.

TREKKING POLES

You will probably meet Appalachian Trail long-distance hikers on your hike. More likely than not, they will be using trekking poles. Long popular in Europe, poles have gained widespread use in the North American hiking community over the past twenty years. Trekking poles are standard equipment for my hikes.

I find them most helpful on descents, particularly the long reaches common to Maine trails, as they provide three points of contact on a downward step as opposed to one. They have saved me from a serious slide or pitch forward more times than I like to count!

On the ascent they offer two more push-off points and stability just at that moment when I shift weight to move up. Poles even have value on level trail by keeping posture upright and the stride efficient. I favor the adjustable-length style for adaptability to terrain, lengthening them for descents, shortening them for ascents. To avoid blisters, I prefer cork grips.

Saddleback Ski Area Route: Saddleback Mountain Lodge, 976 Saddleback Mountain Road

The Saddleback Ski Area is under new ownership effective 2020. Hiker access is expected to continue. Be alert for new signage and hiker information.

South of Rangeley 0.9 mile on Route 4, turn east on Dallas Hill Road, 2.5 miles to Saddleback Mountain Road and 4.6 miles further to the lodge. Watch for new trailhead signage near the lodge. (See below for trailhead details.) Park away from the base lodge in the parking area to the left of the approach road. Do not park in the drop-off circle or behind the building.

- Markers: Expect new signage in 2021. Historically, red and white "Uphill Access" signs have been displayed on conifers to the left of the Upper Gray Ghost and Tri-Color ski trails. These signs begin partway up the slope and may not be visible from the lodge. Ski trail signs (e.g., "Gray Ghost") typically face uphill, for the benefit of descending skiers.
- Maintainer: Saddleback Ski Area.
- Distance to summit: 2.0 miles (4.0 miles RT).
- Points of interest:

  Saddleback base lodge. At the front step, face the mountain; walk across the lawn, ascending to tall grass. A beaten-down trail, or herd path, angles left.

  0.1 Gravel maintenance track, via lodge lawn and herd path across Wheeler slope (former Sandy chairlift line). Turn right on gravel track.

  0.2 Left turn off gravel track to herd path, descending into a draw, ascending through broad opening between tree stands, to Lower Gray Ghost Trail. Sections muddy in wet weather.

  0.3 Lower Gray Ghost Trail. Turn right. Ascend worn path. Pass first Ski Patrol hut at top of chairlift. Watch for "Uphill Access" sign and worn path.

  1.7 Second Ski Patrol hut and second chairlift. Woods trail above hut to right.

  1.8 Brackish tarn, junction with AT immediately beyond. Trail sign lodged in cairn at junction. AT South, right, leads to Highway 4. Turn left (AT North) to reach Saddleback summit.

  2.0 Saddleback summit: 4,120 feet.

This route has become popular with 4,000-Footer hikers because of its short distance compared with other trails. Others choose one of the other routes for their wilder settings. Trail runners like the ski trail option because the lower 1.7 miles, though decidedly steep, do not have the rocks and roots common to many a northern New England hiking trail.

It is common to encounter hikers with dogs on this route. I have brought our chocolate Lab, Moose, here many times. She is always on leash here, never off. Dogs are required to be on leash above tree line (trees 5 feet and shorter) anyway. I use a chest harness for her comfort on steep ground—I do not want to be pulling on her neck! *Dogs are not allowed during the winter season.*

If you are a dog owner, you know about territoriality and the establishment of who is dominant. That may not work well on the mountainside, with children about and other dogs on trail for which this also is unfamiliar territory. A number of times a hiker's dog has headed for the woods in pursuit of a deer, not to be seen again—at least not by the time I returned from my summit hike a few hours later. My suggestion is to practice harnessed hiking at moderate elevations before bringing a dog to a 4,000-Footer.

I use this ski trail route for my own exercise hikes and enjoy the fine northward views available from the get-go because the ski trails are so broadly cut. Saddleback is a wondrous place, and I make time to hike all its routes each year—and create new ones. One of those is to hike Fly Rod Crosby Trail from its northern trailhead near the ski area base lodge, around the mountain, past Eddy Pond, to the Berry Picker's Trail. Next, I head up to the saddle, over to The Horn, back to Saddleback, and down the alpine trail, for one great loop.

Back to the ski trail route, I locate the worn herd path in front of the base lodge, move over the maintenance road, and—on a June day—lupine, lupine, and more lupine. Great stands of lupine extend as far as I can see, up the Wheeler slope, over toward Gray Ghost, and on up the mountainside. Remarkable! I maneuver around mud on lower levels of the ski trails and ascend sharply, passing a ski trail junction or two. An "Uphill Access" sign is affixed to the far left of the trail, which stays right of center for most of the route.

When the level of ascent eases, I turn around for the northward view. The triangular lake straight down is Saddleback Lake. The other triangular body of water beyond is Gull Pond. Double-peaked East Kennebago Mountain rises right of center. West Kennebago is left of center with an angular summit. I come here very early in the day, often before sunup. At this hour mist hangs over the lakes and about the northward valley.

Back to work, with steadier ascent. The trail transitions from Lower Gray Ghost to Upper Gray Ghost. At this writing, there is no sign demarking the two. At the first Ski Patrol hut, Gray Ghost ends, and the trail becomes Tri-Color. A ski area map historically displayed on the hut outside wall has been removed, presumably for updating. My uphill route continues to the right of the hut.

More steepness. The footing becomes loose rock, passable enough, but attention to foot placement and stability is wise. Tri-Color makes an obvious turn diagonal right (I watch for the worn path) to reach the second Ski Patrol hut and the top of the Rangeley chairlift. A time for more views to the north—to the mountains along the Quebec border, including a handful of New England Hundred Highest peaks. Among these are Snow Mountain–Chain of Ponds, Snow Mountain–Cupsuptic, Kennebago Divide, White Cap, and an unnamed peak on the international border unofficially termed Boundary Peak.

Above the hut, the trail is a typical Maine mountain high-ground route: steady ascent through a 3- to 4-foot cut between firs, then krummholz. The trail emerges from the trees and swings left, where a helpful cairn marks the way. How about those flag trees! The Saddleback summit is to the left on the ridge; a delightful tarn is on the right. Beyond that the signpost, new in 2020, marks the junction with the AT.

Turn left on AT North, descend into a shallow col, and then ascend to the summit, with its 360-degree view—and almost certainly a steady wind. Bring out those warm layers in order to enjoy the accomplishment!

Reverse direction for a round-trip hike. Pay close attention to the signpost marking the junction with the ski trail route.

A fine viewing point only 0.2 mile AT North with a much better view of The Horn is available at this summit. Continue for a total of 1.6 miles one way, Saddleback to The Horn (if, that is, your plan and time, daylight, and energy permit).

Caution: Ruffed grouse and other ground-nesting birds make their homes in this high harsh environment in carefully chosen sheltered spots. Dogs must be on a short leash. Stay away from the brush to protect such birds and small mammals. Thank you for caring for this vulnerable terrain!

The Horn of Saddleback

Range: Saddleback (on some maps, "The Rangeley Mountains")
Location: Madrid Township
Elevation: 4,041 feet
Rank: 12
Elevation gain: Varies by trailhead and whether hiking only The Horn or both Saddleback and The Horn. The Horn only via Berry Picker's Trail approach: 2,400 feet. Hikers summiting Saddleback (2,500-foot gain) and The Horn on the same hike will experience a further 600-foot elevation loss and gain between the two peaks. An out-and-back hike will double those figures, for an additional elevation gain of 1,200 feet and a total elevation gain for a Saddleback–The Horn hike of 3,700 feet.
Lands traversed: Appalachian Trail Corridor (the Fly Rod Crosby and Saddleback ski area approaches cross private land)
Nearby supply town: Rangeley
Fee: None
Maps: USGS Saddleback Mountain, Redington; MATC AT Strip Map #6, Maine Highway 27 to Maine Highway 17; DeLorme Maine Atlas Map #29, 1-E, 2-E (A Fly Rod Crosby Trail map is useful to access Berry Picker's Trail and other Saddleback-area footpaths.)

The Horn of Saddleback rises as a distinctive cone 1.6 miles AT North of the Saddleback peak. The long col between the two peaks bears the distinctive saddle likeness that gives the Saddleback Range its name. Some of the best views of the saddle

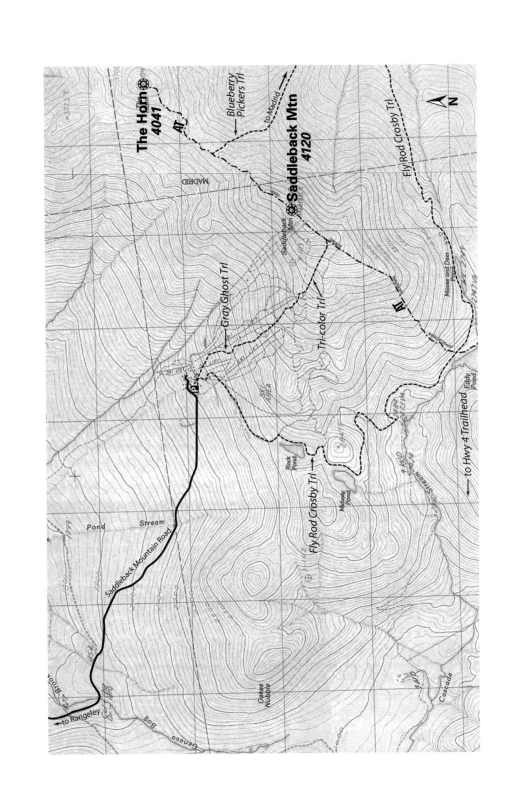

conformation are from the Sandy River intervale north of the towns of Strong and Phillips.

The open summit provides 360-degree views, from the Quebec border to the sea, Mt. Washington to Katahdin. Enjoy the added benefit of a close-up look at Saddleback itself and close inspection of the northeast-lying peaks of sub-4,000-foot Saddleback Junior and Poplar Ridge and the cut of Orbeton Canyon. Beyond these is the north–south sweep of five more 4,000-Footers: North and South Crocker, Redington, Sugarloaf, Spaulding, and Abraham. For identification, carry a map that encompasses all these high peaks.

The summit cone may remind hikers of other New England 4,000-Footer coned peaks, such as Mts. Liberty and Fume in the White Mountains, Camel's Hump in the Green Mountains, and West Peak on the Bigelow Range, 33 AT trail miles to the north. The surrounding ridge is a magnificent alpine zone, where abundant cotton sedge shakes in ridgetop winds. And does that wind blow! On my most recent trip, I discovered a new summit sign, installed in 2020, replacing the former sign carried off by winter winds.

The Horn is a long day hike, drawing far fewer day hikers than Saddleback, rendering it a place of solitude on most days. I enjoy lingering here to take in, amid the silence, the rare look it offers into the very heart of the Western Mountains of Maine.

- Single-peak itinerary: The Horn may be ascended as a single destination by way of the Berry Picker's Trail and the AT, without including the Saddleback summit in the itinerary.
- Multiple-peak itineraries: Saddleback and The Horn are often combined on a single day hike, by way of the AT North from Highway 4; Berry Picker's Trail with a hike AT South to Saddleback and AT North to The Horn; or the Saddleback ski area trail route to Saddleback and AT North to The Horn.
- Approach trail: Saddleback Range Trail/AT (see "Saddleback Mountain" entry, above).
- Distance to summit of The Horn: 7.3 miles (14.6 miles RT).
- Points of interest:
    AT trailhead, Highway 4 Sandy River footbridge.
    5.7 Saddleback summit.
    5.9 Knob AT North of Saddleback.
    6.5 Berry Picker's Trail (see above).
    7.3 The Horn summit.

I describe the AT North route to The Horn by starting with a description from Saddleback summit. On many a Saddleback hike I step over to the knob 0.2 mile AT North of the Saddleback peak for a good look at The Horn and beyond, take a break, and savor the quiet. To continue across the saddle between the two, I descend sharply, with a few long step-downs, maneuvering carefully with the aid of trekking poles. Still above tree line, still in the alpine zone, still among erratics, krummholz, and alpine flora—and the occasional junco flitting from fir to fir.

Beyond, I notice a patch of purple-blue, a small tarn two-thirds of the way across the saddle, an outcropping cliff beyond that, and at the farthest extent of the saddle, a perceptible worn path through the krummholz leading to the summit of The Horn. Continuing descent brings me to a stand of higher fir, one more long step-down, and the junction with the Berry Picker's Trail, which enters from the right (south), 0.8 mile from the Saddleback peak. A new sign (2016) announces mileage points on the BPT. A one-page laminated description of the trail shares the signpost.

Heading AT North, I leave the fir stand, emerge onto more open ledge, erratic boulders scattered about, pass the tarn, rippling in the wind, and ascend steadily. An iron ladder aids with what would otherwise be quite an upward scramble over nearly vertical rock. The trail zigzags to maneuver around the outcrop I had viewed earlier. I pause at its upper edge to gain a good view of the upper reaches of the Berry Picker's Trail—open ledges and that distinctive great erratic.

More steady climbing, and I am at the top! The summit cairn sports a new sign. On my most recent previous hike to The Horn, the old sign was gone, and the post looked weathered indeed. I look to the north and northwest, the direction of Canada, whence come prevailing winds and many a winter storm. No higher ground rises in that direction until the Canadian Rockies! The full sweep of winter hits the Saddleback Range full tilt!

I have passed this way in a sleet storm in July. On another hike to the range, I opted not to continue to The Horn on an October day when a high-elevation snowstorm whipped the peaks, piled snow up to two feet deep, and staggered me as I hiked. That day, in the surrounding valleys, sun was shining on the fall foliage! No such drama on this day. The sun is bright and the sky clear, the view extends to the horizon, and the wind is comfortably cool.

Nearby Trails
Saddleback Ski Area Route (see "Saddleback Mountain" section for details)
The AT North route to The Horn beyond the Saddleback summit is the same for both the Highway 4 AT Trailhead route and the Saddleback ski area route. Once at the Saddleback summit, continue AT North.

- Distance to summit: From Saddleback Mountain, 1.6 miles (3.2 RT); from Saddleback ski lodge, 3.6 miles (7.2 miles RT).
- Points of interest:
     0.2 Knob beyond Saddleback summit, with good view of The Horn.
     0.8 Berry Picker's Trail.
     1.6 The Horn summit.

Hikers continuing to The Horn make a way over striking alpine terrain, descending nearly 500 feet of elevation, and gaining that back in the final ascent to the summit. That feat accomplished, the reverse hike repeats the process. I treasure my times on this section of the Saddleback ridge. The setting is striking—with these two imposing peaks looming at either end of the long col, broad stretches of glacially striated ledge, a tiny tarn, and a scattering of glacial erratics.

The AT North beyond Saddleback Mountain summit descends steadily, even sharply in spots, with occasional long reaches. On a clear day, the dramatic sight of the pyramid peak of The Horn is all but a distraction. I alternate between watching my feet and taking in the view.

The junction with Berry Picker's Trail, halfway across the saddle, is in a shady spot that offers some relief on a hot day—yes, we do have such days!

Beyond this junction the footpath moderates, descending more gradually, passing the tarn, and reaching the low point in the saddle. The trail ascends steadily, negotiating a way up a long-reach boulder with an iron ladder as an assist and around a cliff edge via a circumventing twist in the trail. From the cliff top I trace the route of the Berry Picker's Trail along the boundary edges and have a direct look at the great glacial boulder near the top of those ledges.

From here, I have a good view of my destination: the sharply oriented summit. Up, up—and I am there! Beyond, on AT North, lies Saddleback Junior and the 4,000-Footers of Spaulding and Sugarloaf, and to the southeast is the long, imposing ridge of Mt. Abraham. To the northeast lies another cluster: Redington Mountain and South and North Crocker.

On my latest ascent I find a new summit sign, installed by Maine Appalachian Trail Club volunteers. In earlier days, I had hiked here to find the wording on the old sign all but obliterated by the work of the wind. It is likely that this former, weather-worn sign, lifted by the wind from its post, now lies in pieces far down the mountainside, in the direction of Orbeton Canyon.

With a combination of gratitude for the day and reluctance to leave, I depart the rocky summit of The Horn to descend back into the saddle, my first steps back toward home.

Berry Picker's Trail to The Horn

The Horn may be ascended as a one-peak hike via the Berry Picker's Trail without summiting Saddleback Mountain. Upon reaching the intersection of BPT with the AT, hikers may turn right (AT North) to travel an additional 0.8 mile to the summit.

See the description above of the route from Saddleback summit to The Horn summit for a description of features of the saddle along the way.

For the Berry Picker's Trail from the Winship Stream trailhead to the AT on the Saddleback ridge, see the previous section about Saddleback Mountain approach trails.

- Distance to The Horn summit: 2.5 miles (5.0 miles RT). Add to this distance the 1.4 miles (2.8 miles RT) Fly Rod Crosby Trail and snowmobile trail ITS 84/89/Fly Rod Crosby Trail walk from the parking area by the planked Conant Stream bridge to reach the Berry Picker's Trail at Winship Stream. Total from Conant bridge parking: 3.9 miles (7.8 miles RT).
- Points of interest:
    Winship Stream trailhead for Berry Picker's Trail.
    1.7 Junction with AT on Saddleback ridge.
    2.5 The Horn summit via AT North.

Welcoming an alternate perspective on the Saddleback Range and the quiet remoteness of the south slope of the range, I have ascended The Horn by the Berry Picker's Trail. On other days I have summited both The Horn and Saddleback on the same hike, using the Berry Picker's Trail as principal access. Such a hike involves out and back, ridge to summits, back to ridge, but I relish the stark beauty of this setting and am pleased to enjoy this alternate route.

Mt. Abraham Range

The Mt. Abraham Range stretches nearly 5 miles, north to south, a largely trailless felsenmeer (sea of rock) ridge, punctuated by krummholz—swaths of black spruce, balsam fir, and gnarled, yellowed white birch. Only the north summit, a former fire-tower peak, is touched by maintained trails. Some adventurers have bushwhacked to the Middle and South Peaks (the latter also known as East Peak), but the way is decidedly rough going.

This rambling range is one of my favorites. With its interior location, main trailhead approach by way of rough-passage logging roads, and massive rock fields covering the high ground, Abraham exudes wildness. In a mountain region that is largely uncrowded, Abraham is singularly so. In many years of hiking the mountain, I have yet to meet another hiker at the summit, except for my own hiking companions.

Mt. Abraham (a.k.a. Mt. Abram)

Range: Mt. Abraham
Location: Mt. Abram Township
Elevation: 4,050 feet
Rank: 10 (tie with South Crocker)
Elevation gain: 2,900 feet (Fire Warden Trail)
Rank: 12
Lands traversed: Mt. Abraham Maine Public Reserved Land

Nearby supply town: Kingfield
Fees: None
Maps: Mt. Abraham; Maine Bureau of Public Lands, Mt. Abraham (https://maine.gov); MATC AT Strip Map #6, Maine Highway 27 to Maine Highway 17; DeLorme Maine Atlas Map #29: 3-E, 4-E, 5-E

Mt. Abraham is often referred to locally as Mt. Abram—some road signage bears that local name. Trail signs depict the full name.

The views to other 4,000-Footers, north to the Appalachian Trail (AT) summits of Saddleback, Spaulding, and Sugarloaf, and beyond these toward the Crockers and Redington, are extraordinary—a rare opportunity to step back a bit from these nearby ranges and regard them from a high, south-lying perspective. On either side of the range, the landscape falls away to river valleys deeply cut at their origin, more gently sloped at lower elevations: Rapid Stream Valley and the Carrabassett Valley to

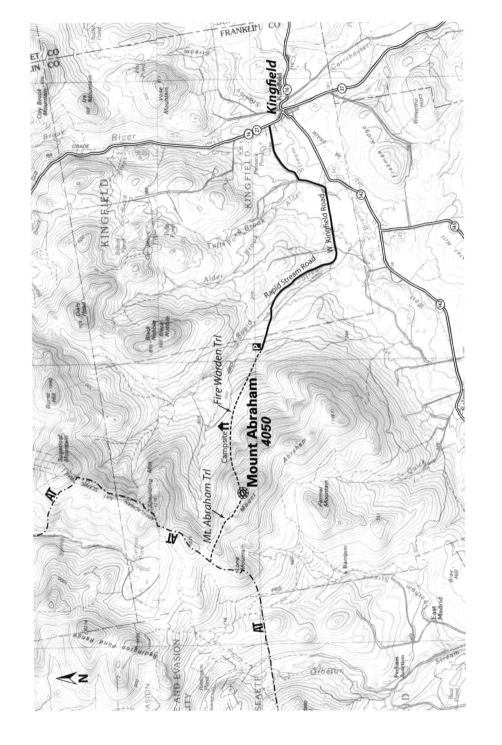

the east, the valleys of Orbeton Stream and the Sandy River to the west. The two watercourses join at the Kennebec River, 60 miles to the south.

The origin of the Mt. Abraham name is uncertain. The township to the north, now part of Carrabassett Valley, was once named Jerusalem Township, and a Salem Township lies to the southwest. These two names, along with Abraham, have biblical roots. Yet a history of the Rangeley area refers to a landowner named Abraham, who went by the shortened version of Abram, and both versions of the name have been applied to the mountain and region for many years.

The rock rubble at higher elevations requires careful foot placement. It can be slippery in wet conditions and impassable when ice is present—which may occur in spring and fall shoulder seasons and on occasional summer days. Expect strong winds as the norm. A crude rock windbreak has been shaped near the summit by hikers. The high ground is completely exposed and should be avoided in storm conditions.

- Single-peak itinerary: Fire Warden Trail, Rapid Stream Valley to summit, 4.0 miles (8.0 miles RT).
- Multiple-peak itineraries: Elevation gain and ruggedness of terrain and trail limit the number of hikers who combine another 4,000-Footer with Abraham when hiking from Rapid Stream Valley. Some hikers continue on the Mt. Abraham trail to AT North, thence to Spaulding Mountain, and return, but that amounts to 15.6 miles round-trip and the summiting of Mt. Abraham twice. (See "Backpacking Maine's 4,000-Footers" in the "Out of the Ordinary" section of this book for itineraries that shorten the day hike by tenting overnight at the Fire Warden Trail campsite or incorporate the Mt. Abraham spur trail from the AT and continue to the Saddleback Range to the southwest or the Sugarloaf-Spaulding Range to the northeast.)
- Trail/trailhead: Fire Warden Trail; Mt. Abraham spur trail.
- Markers: Blue blazes.
- Maintainer: MATC.

Trails
Fire Warden Trail

In Kingfield, 0.5 mile north of the intersection of Highways 27 and 16 at Carrabassett River Bridge, turn left (west) on West Kingfield Road (corner at Jordan Lumber Co., diagonally across Highway 27 from Tranten's Market). See the Maine's High Peaks directional sign, "Mt. Abram Trailhead," on the right side of Highway 27. Pavement ends at 3.3 miles. Continue on gravel surface to the four-way intersection at 3.4 miles. Go straight on Rapid Stream Road (sign). This road has been repaired from extensive flooding damage in 2011 from Hurricane Irene but is rough in spots. No speed limit is posted, but 10 to 15 mph is prudent to avoid a flat tire and suspension wear and tear. Be alert for those walking, on bicycles, or on ATVs. Rapid Stream comes into view at mile 4.1 on the left. At mile 5.7, see a snowmobile trail sign for Interconnected Trail System (ITS) Connector 115, as this is a snowmobile route in winter. At 5.9 miles reach a major road/snowmobile trail junction. Bear diagonal left (snowmobile signs to Salem, Phillips) to reach the first Rapid Stream Bridge at mile 6.0 and the second in another 100 feet. (These and a second bridge beyond were washed away during Hurricane Irene in 2011; they were replaced by 2016.) After crossing the second bridge, turn right at a junction (see Mt. Abraham Trail directional sign). Follow this sometimes-rough road 0.5 mile to a junction where the parking area is on the immediate left. No facilities. The trailhead (sign) is directly across from the approach road you have just traveled. It may be partially obscured by nearby brush, but the trail, once located, is well worn and clear to follow.

- Distance to summit: 4.0 miles (8.0 miles RT).
- Points of interest:
  Trailhead parking.
  1.3 Gravel road above Norton Brook.
  2.5 Last water (stream).
  2.6 Campsite with privy.
  3.4 Tree line.
  4.0 Mt. Abraham summit: 4,050 feet; junction with Mt. Abraham spur trail to Appalachian Trail.

A hiking companion and I are pleased to find the Rapid Stream Road in good shape, bridges as well, and the final 0.5-mile approach road to the Fire Warden trailhead smooth going. Previous winters had been long ones, hard on roads. Both the road and the Fire Warden Trail show evidence of recent upgrades. The trail has been

Late one summer afternoon, I approach the Mt. Abraham summit via the Mt. Abraham spur trail from the AT, scramble across the rock field that rings the summit, and emerge on top to watch the sun make its first noticeable slip toward the horizon, shaded valleys on either side rendered velvet in the shadows of late day.

I take a seat, alone on the summit—or so I thought—as the light diminishes, casts new shadows over the valley below, and brightens the heights of Saddleback Range with an amber hue. In this moment I am completely alone. From nearby sedge a grasshopper leaps, lands on my shoulder, and positions itself looking sunward. I make not a move. Neither does the grasshopper.

So it is that the two of us, my grasshopper companion and I, remain there for a good long time, quiet, not moving, simply looking in the direction of the low late-afternoon sun.

notoriously wet in its lower half, but major sections have been relocated to higher, drier ground, and water bars and rock steps have been installed to manage runoff and avoid trail erosion.

We ascend gradually at first, and then more steadily, roughly following the now grown-in route of the old Fire Warden cabin road. After crossing a gravel road above Norton Brook, and another rock-hop stream, at 2.6 miles we reach the MATC campsite (tenting only; water from nearby stream).

The grade steepens in the final 1.4 miles to the summit, reaching tree line 0.9 mile from the campsite. A sign cautions hikers to tread carefully in the fragile alpine environment; it also reads, "Appalachian Trail." We are *not* on the AT, which is 2.2 miles distant, but the message still applies. Upward we scramble for the last 0.5 mile, over the summit-circling sea of rock—to take in a view from Old Speck to the Crockers and south over the rugged Abraham Range to the foothills beyond.

Mt. Abraham Spur Trail

The interior trailhead (trailhead sign) is not approachable by road. Most common use is by AT hikers summiting Mt. Abraham on multiday backpack trips between Highways 4 and 27. The spur trail departs from AT North 7.2 miles from the Poplar Ridge campsite and 1.0 mile south of the Spaulding Mountain campsite.

- Distance to Mt. Abraham summit: 1.7 miles (3.4 miles RT).
- Points of interest:
     AT junction with Mt. Abraham Trail.
     0.8 First knob and rock field.
     1.0 Second knob and rock field.
     1.7 Mt. Abraham summit: 4,050 feet; junction with Fire Warden Trail to Rapid Stream parking area.

While hiking an extended section of the AT, north from Grafton Notch, I make my first use of the Mt. Abraham spur trail to reach the summit. On previous ascents of Mt. Abraham, I have hiked the Fire Warden Trail. It is a sunny late afternoon in August, a cooling time of day. Following a round-trip hike to the summit, I plan to tent at Spaulding Mountain campsite.

The trailhead, on the right side of the trail as I hike AT North, is well marked with the customary Maine Appalachian Trail Club (MATC) sign. Directly across from the trail, on the left, an overgrown road leads into Caribou Valley. The first section of the Mt. Abraham Trail is a continuation of that road on the east side of the ridge, where it descends through firs to a col. When hiking the reverse of this route in late May one year, I encountered knee-deep snow in the cols, although I found no snow at all along the Fire Warden Trail and at the Mt. Abraham summit on that spring day.

From this low point the trail ascends the first of two rocky knobs, levels, and ascends the second, higher knob with views south to the valleys of Perham and Barnjum Streams and the intermediate peak of 3,200-foot Farmer Mountain, which lies due south of the Mt. Abraham summit. Farmer Mountain blocks a view to the once busy farming community of East Madrid, which had a school, a post office, a cattle ranch, and a good number of farms established there to take advantage of the southern exposure. A branch of the Narrow Gauge Railroad ran to the lower slopes of Mt. Abraham to carry timber to mills farther south.

The remaining 0.4 mile is a steady uphill over rocky open ground to the open summit. Middle Peak of Mt. Abraham is similarly rock strewn. A lightning-caused forest fire burned a wide area around Middle Peak in 2017. Given how fragile alpine growth is, that portion of the range is likely to remain rocky, with little plant life, for the foreseeable future. It will be instructive to watch.

I am on the summit by myself, the sun lower in the sky, rich early-evening light on my face and the surrounding rocky high ground. Westward peaks throw lengthening shadows into the valley below. Fir and spruce take on a hue of deep, dark blue. I sit by the summit cairn, enjoy the solitude for a time, rise, and head back to the AT and on to camp.

Sugarloaf-Spaulding Range

Reportedly once referred to as part of the Mt. Abraham Range and later as one Sugarloaf Range, this north–south stretch of high ground, with two 4,000-Footers, does not have a single name by consensus. I use the term "Sugarloaf-Spaulding Range" to acknowledge what is there—two of Maine's highest peaks, connected by a ridge of 3,500-plus feet.

Each peak, for different reasons, is not commonly thought of as a hiking destination. The original intent of the Four-Thousand-Footer Club applies here—to encourage hikers to visit terrain they otherwise might not and thereby discover what fine hiking destinations these are.

Sugarloaf has the third-highest summit in Maine and is the highest peak between Mt. Washington and Katahdin. The views over the cluster of neighboring 4,000-Footers are superb, particularly of the lengthy Bigelow Range to the north. The mountain is famous as home to the world-class Sugarloaf alpine ski resort. Sugarloaf has hosted many international snow-sport competitions and is home to snowboard cross Olympic gold medalist Seth Wescott.

Hikers may ascend the north slopes using alpine ski trails or a maintenance track to reach the summit, marked by a large cairn, which rises in the midst of communications towers and associated buildings, a helipad, and facilities at the upper end of ski lifts. Nevertheless, the view is worthy of the ascent, and in summer there are many points along the way on a summit hike where hikers may enjoy unbroken views amid a multitude of wildflowers—lupine, brown-eyed Susans, daisies, Queen Anne's lace.

The south side of the mountain, by contrast, is approached by a typical high mountain trail, ascending trailside past balsam fir, bunchberry, and bluebead lily and a high-elevation spring.

The section of the Appalachian Trail (AT) that connects Sugarloaf and Spaulding is historic, as it passes the point where a Civilian Conservation Corps (CCC) crew in 1937 completed the last section of the Appalachian Trail. A plaque honors that achievement.

Wooded though it may be, the summit of Spaulding offers lookout points to Sugarloaf, the Crockers and Redington, and the Sugarloaf Range, that are exceptional.

Spaulding Mountain

Range: Sugarloaf-Spaulding massif. Some sources indicate that the entire range was once considered all part of Sugarloaf. Although connected by a 2-mile ridge, the two peaks are now usually referred to separately. This and neighboring ranges are labeled on some maps as the "Longfellow Mountains"; this term (not widely used locally) was once applied to the inland mountains of Maine more generally.
Location: Mt. Abram Township
Elevation: 4,010 feet

Rank: 13/14 (tied with Redington Mountain)
Elevation gain: 2,450 feet
Lands traversed: Appalachian Trail Corridor
Nearby supply towns: Kingfield, Carrabassett Valley
Fees: None
Maps: USGS Sugarloaf Mountain; MATC AT Strip Map #6, Maine Highway 27 to Maine Highway 17; DeLorme Maine Atlas Map #29, 3-D, 4-D

One of the more interior of the Maine 4,000-Footers, Spaulding rises south of Sugarloaf as the highest point between Sugarloaf and the Saddleback Range and offers good views toward each of these neighbors. Seen from the intervales along Highway 27 from Kingfield south, it has an imposing cone profile. Although Spaulding was added to the 4,000-Footer list over twenty years ago, in 1998, as a result of improved elevation-determination methods, the old elevation of 3,988 feet remains displayed on a sign a few feet from the true summit.

Although the summit is wooded, there are excellent lookout points only steps away from the peak. To the northeast, there is an outstanding look at the wild south-facing

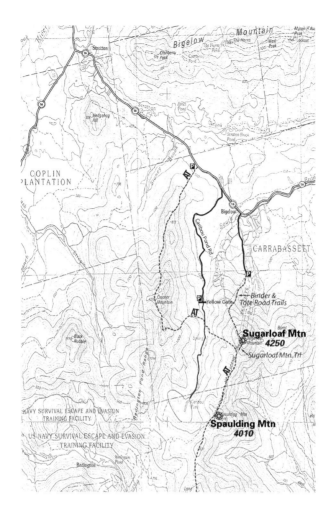

slope of Sugarloaf and east into the valley where rise the intermediate-level peaks of Owl's Head and Black Nubble. To the east of Sugarloaf, a saddle extends to the rocky summit of Burnt Mountain. Another viewing point looks over the Caribou Valley toward the Crocker Range and Redington Mountain. Yet one more lookout, to the west, takes in the Saddleback Range from a rare downrange perspective. Linger at each of these points. Spaulding is worth more than a tag!

The origin of the name is obscure. Many a Maine mountain earned its first name from an early landowner who purchased a great swath of forestland, of which mountain peaks were but a small part and of limited interest. Harvesting and skidding out high-terrain timber would be difficult, and such ground was not suitable for agriculture or homesteading. As time passed, lands changed hands. Some names were retained. Spaulding is an old New England name, attached to historical events in New Hampshire and found in Maine communities today. An ancestral Spaulding is the likely source for this 4,000-Footer's name.

- Single-peak itinerary: Spaulding may be summited by itself as a round-trip day hike from Caribou Pond Road.
- Multiple-peak itinerary: Sugarloaf and Spaulding may be combined in a day hike, using the Sugarloaf Mountain spur trail to ascend Sugarloaf from the south. Hikers who climb Sugarloaf via the ski trail route may continue south on the Sugarloaf Mountain spur to meet the AT South and continue to Spaulding. Spaulding may be added to a day hike of Mt. Abraham by use of the Mt. Abraham spur between that peak and the AT.
- Trailheads: AT South: Caribou Pond Road Gate (a.k.a. Yellow Gate), 3.9 miles south from Maine Highway 27 serves as the trailhead. This gravel road is also known locally, and represented on some maps and in some guidebooks, as the Caribou Valley Road. It is located off Maine Highway 27, 1.0 mile north of the Sugarloaf Access Road and 1.7 miles south of the AT trailhead in Wyman Township. Make a sharp left turn near the crest of Bigelow Hill. Watch for a green "Caribou Pond Road" sign, new in 2019.
- This gravel road was upgraded in 2018 with new ditching, bridge and culvert repair, widening of the roadway, and grading. Previously it had been prone to erosion and seasonal washouts. There are blue mile markers at miles 1, 2, and 3. The road crosses Weyerhaeuser Corporation land.
- The so-called Yellow Gate serves as trailhead for Spaulding, Sugarloaf (south side); South Crocker and North Crocker from the south; and Redington Mountain. Parking; no facilities; no sign. Hike 0.5 mile to AT crossing (no sign), marked by cairns and white blazes. Turn left on AT South to ford the South Branch of the Carrabassett River. Continue toward Spaulding Mountain.
- Markings: White blazes.
- Maintainer: MATC.
- Distance to summit: 5.0 miles (10.0 miles RT).
- Points of interest:
  Caribou Pond Road Yellow Gate and parking.
  0.5 AT crossing of Caribou Pond Road—left for AT South.
  0.6 Ford of South Branch, Carrabassett River (dangerous at high water).
  2.0 Viewing point over Sugarloaf Cirque.
  2.3 Stream.
  2.8 Sugarloaf Mountain Trail.
  4.2 CCC plaque.
  4.9 Junction Spaulding Mountain spur trail.
  5.0 Spaulding Mountain summit: 4,010 feet.

AT South

Beyond the Yellow Gate, my hiking party walks the Caribou Pond Road, arrives at the AT crossing, and heads left to descend to the noisy South Branch of the Carrabassett River. On this mid-July day, the water level is moderate, and we ford without incident. At high water the ford can be *dangerous.* The route parallels the river at first. The grade soon steepens, and the trail employs rare (in the Maine mountains) switchbacks to negotiate small cliffs largely hidden by tree growth.

Two miles from the trailhead, the route makes a sharp left turn at an overlook into Sugarloaf Cirque, a great basin carved by glacial activity. This cirque is a near mirror image of Crocker Cirque, visible to the north across the valley. The best views of both are from the trail; the valley is hidden from the sight of highway travelers on nearby Highway 27.

The trail moderates as it approaches the Sugarloaf Mountain Trail junction (sign). Distance to the summit is 0.6 mile. When my destination is Spaulding, I usually save summiting Sugarloaf for the return hike. In that way, I reach the farthest point of my journey first. If I am delayed for some reason and run out of time to hike Sugarloaf, I will have a shorter hike on a future day when I return. There is a boxed spring halfway up the trail on the left, a rare high-elevation water source. *Note:* The junction sign refers to the ski lift line as the route to descend Sugarloaf to the base lodge and Sugarloaf Village. However, the recommended route is by Tote Road or the Binder Trail, not the lift line near the center of the mountain slope, which passes over cliff formations and is difficult to descend.

We continue toward Spaulding, crossing through high-elevation boggy ground and by extensive blowdowns. This ridge is blowdown prone—an observation by early AT through-hikers Earl Shaffer in 1948 and Emma Gatewood in 1955. There appears to be just enough soil depth and residual moisture to produce stands of fir 10 to 16 inches in diameter—and enough beating by strong winter winds to blow them over. That contest continues.

The trail is refreshingly level, another Maine mountain rarity. Viewing points to the east provide fine looks into Rapid Stream Valley and toward intermediate peaks of Owl's Head and Black Nubble. We reach the CCC marker memorializing the completion of the AT near this point. The plaque is affixed to an erratic boulder in a small clearing. Good place to stop and ponder that work.

On to the Spaulding spur trail. A small sign indicates 150 yards to the summit. The steep grade makes the distance seem a bit longer than that. We reach the small summit clearing, an old sign listing elevation as 3,988 feet (not the current 4,010 feet), and spread out to check the various viewing points: Sugarloaf and its sub-4,000-foot neighbor Burnt Mountain, the Crocker Range and Redington, and the Saddleback Range. We have reached the very heart of 4,000-foot country in Maine.

WHO BUILT THIS?

Who built this trail? A bronze plaque, installed on a trailside boulder 3.5 miles south of the Caribou Pond Road and 0.7 mile north of Spaulding Mountain spur trail, commemorates the noble work of the Civilian Conservation Corps. Between 1933 and 1942, some three million CCC workers built park access roads, trails, and public facilities and engaged in hundreds of other rural infrastructure projects. During a time of 25 percent unemployment in the Great Depression, these workers built rural infrastructure that has economic value to rural communities to this day, earned income to provide for their families, and developed work skills and experience that enabled them to succeed in the job market as the economy improved. In 1937, a work crew completed the final section of the Georgia–Maine Appalachian Trail on this ridge between Sugarloaf Mountain and Spaulding Mountain. It is because of such efforts that you and I have this footpath.

Sugarloaf Mountain

Range: Sugarloaf-Spaulding massif
Location: Carrabassett Valley
Elevation: 4,250 feet
Rank: 3
Elevation gain: Varies with route; 2,250 feet
Land units traversed: Appalachian Trail Corridor; Sugarloaf ski area; private land (varies by trail)
Nearby supply towns: Kingfield, Carrabassett Valley

Fees: During alpine ski season, Uphill Access Pass ($10) from Guest Services office on the mountain
Maps: USGS Sugarloaf Mountain; MATC AT Strip Map #6, Maine Highway 27 to Maine Highway 17; DeLorme Maine Atlas Map #29: 3-D, 4-D; Sugarloaf ski trail map (available at Guest Services, the Sugarloaf Hotel, and https://sugarloaf.com) (*Note:* Tote Road and Binder Trail are located to the right of center on the ski map display as parallel dogleg routes to the summit area.)

Sugarloaf is the third-highest peak in Maine and rises on the second-highest mountain mass, or massif, in the state. For this reason it has mistakenly been referred to as Maine's second-highest peak, although that designation belongs to Hamlin Peak in Baxter State Park. Views to the north and east toward the Bigelow Range and beyond

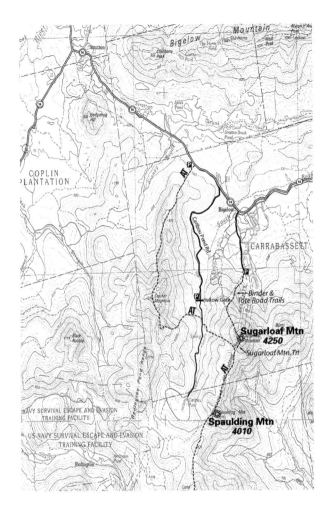

in the direction of Moosehead Lake and the mountains that rise along the Maine-Quebec border are breathtaking. Katahdin rises on the far northeast skyline.

The name of the mountain derives from the conical shape of molded sugar, the form in which refinement was completed and the sugar marketed until the late 1800s. There are six mountains in Maine containing the name Sugarloaf, including an 1,860-foot peak near Shin Pond in northern Penobscot County, which offers a fine view southwesterly of the mountains of Baxter State Park.

The north side is the location of the Sugarloaf ski area. The complex on that side of the mountain includes the base lodge, restaurants and shops, condominiums and homes, a chapel, a golf course, an indoor recreation and fitness center, and multiple offices and support buildings. The summit area includes communication towers, a helipad, and ski lift buildings.

The south side, by contrast, is undeveloped, wild, and forested with fir, spruce, and alpine white birch. Summit views in this direction extend to the south-lying

4,000-Footers of Spaulding, Abraham, Saddleback and The Horn, and Old Speck. Mt. Washington and the Presidential Range ride the southwestern horizon. This view is truly outstanding, as the next higher 4,000-Footer to the south is Middle Carter (4,610 feet) in the Carter-Moriah Range, 110 AT trail miles distant.

Are you a trail runner? The annual Sugarloaf Uphill, held on the second weekend in October, ascends 2,400 vertical feet over a distance of approximately 2 miles (details and registration: https://sugarloaf.com). This could be the quickest way to bag a Maine 4,000-Footer!

- Single-peak itineraries: Sugarloaf may be summited from the south as a day hike by ascending the AT from Caribou Pond Road, AT South, and the Sugarloaf Mountain Trail. From the north, hike the Binder or Tote Road alpine ski trails from Sugarloaf Village.
- Multiple-peak itineraries: A Sugarloaf hike may be combined with an ascent of Spaulding Mountain. Choose one of the above ascent routes. From the summit of Sugarloaf, descend south on Sugarloaf Mountain Trail to meet AT South. Continue AT South to Spaulding Mountain spur trail. (*Note:* When descending from the summit cairn, look for the blue blazes [some faded] that mark the way of the Sugarloaf Mountain spur trail. The trail passes to the right of the helipad to enter the woods, where the cutout of the trail becomes readily apparent and the blue blazes continue.)
- Approach trails: AT South/Sugarloaf Mountain Trail; see entry for Spaulding Mountain (above) for approach via AT South from Caribou Pond Road; Sugarloaf Mountain Trail.
- Markers: Blue blazes, cairns.
- Maintainer: MATC.

Nearby Trails
Sugarloaf Mountain Trail/Appalachian Trail South from Caribou Pond Road

What is called the Sugarloaf Mountain Trail is the short, 0.6-mile spur that ascends the summit cone from the Appalachian Trail on the south side of Sugarloaf. Most of the ascent mileage from this side is on the AT South of Caribou Pond Road, described above in the "Spaulding Mountain" section. Hikers may find the Sugarloaf Mountain Trail name confusing, expecting a base-to-summit route by that name. In sum, hikers from the south approach the mountain via the AT and finish the ascent by this spur. Those who hike from the north, via the ski area, do not use this spur to reach the top, as the alpine ski trails extend all the way to the summit.

The south side of Sugarloaf is one of my favorite locales in the Maine mountains. When I climb out of Caribou Valley to the summit, the route includes a river ford, a muscle-burning sharp ascent, a cliff-side view down into plummeting Sugarloaf

Cirque, a short section of nearly level high-forest trail, a trailside spring only 0.25 mile from the very top, and an alpine summit!

This high-elevation spur has the feel of high-country trails in the White Mountains I recall from my youth as the pathway ascends in a cut through head-high thick fir, open sky above and through those trees, summit winds swishing about.

Day hikers tend to choose the ski slope route over the more rugged AT pathway, with the result that over decades of hiking I have yet to meet another party on this spur trail. Balsam fir, sphagnum and rock moss, juncos flitting amid the fir—this is a sweet spot. The trail breaks out of the firs to rocky open ground and the complex of summit structures above. A summit cairn marks the very top. There are striking long views to be had, among them my favorite: a look back over the 4,000-Footers south and west—Spaulding, Abraham, Saddleback and The Horn, Redington, and the Crockers.

- Distance to summit: From Caribou Pond Road Yellow Gate: 3.4 miles (6.8 miles RT).
- Points of interest:
    Caribou Pond Road Yellow Gate.
    0.5 AT crossing; AT South.
    0.6 South Branch Carrabassett River (ford).
    2.8 Sugarloaf Mountain Trail.
    3.1 Water/boxed spring.
    3.4 Sugarloaf summit: 4,250 feet.

Binder and Tote Road Trails

At the prominent blinking light on Maine Highway 27, 15 miles north of Kingfield, turn left (south) on the Sugarloaf Access Road. Drive uphill approximately 2 miles to the broad parking area below the multistory Sugarloaf Hotel near the end of the road. Park in the lot by the Richard Bell Chapel.

Walk south, up through the village, to reach the base of the Binder Trail, a gravel maintenance road in summer on a diagonal rise to the right (west). No hiker trailhead sign.

Binder is a gravel track to the summit and is my preference for ascent: better uphill footing, westward views, and morning shade.

Tote Road may be preferred for descent: grassy slope, striking northward views. Views of the Bigelow Range are particularly impressive from Tote Road, which is not a true road, but rather a broad and steep ski trail. This north side is developed, sure, but I go for the view and don't let myself get distracted. I have given mountain running a try on Sugarloaf! I did not keep up a running pace for long and spent most of the way in a double-time stride. In the end, it was different and fun, and I am glad

I did it. Take the opportunity to make the most of it. Each approach to this high summit has something compelling to offer. Hike both!

- Markers: Uphill-facing ski trail signs.
- Maintainer: Sugarloaf Ski Resort.
- Distance to summit: 2.2 miles (4.4 miles RT).
- Points of interest:
  - Parking lot by Richard Bell Chapel, below Sugarloaf Hotel.
  - 0.1 Village complex.
  - 0.2 Bottom of Binder Trail and Tote Road routes above the village complex.
  - 2.2 Sugarloaf summit: 4,250 feet.

I am on trail by 7:30 a.m., and the indicators are that this early July day will be a hot one. The sun has been up for over two hours; the air is warm, not much of a breeze. In shorts and a T-shirt, but with warm layers in the day pack, I walk up through the Sugarloaf Village to the bottom of converging ski slopes. Binder is to my right; Tote Road is ahead. The two are separated by a line of maples, white birch, and fir that leaves a shadow on Binder—making it my choice for ascent.

The route is a dogleg, heading west at first, angling southward at a point halfway up the mountain. Spur road openings to the west provide views toward the Crocker Range, which become more extensive the higher I go. There are openings to the east as well for maintenance personnel to access the snowmaking system on Tote Road and other trails. I avoid these to hold to the shade of Binder. In the final 0.5 mile, Binder passes underneath Cinder Hoe chairlift, and the grade steepens. I emerge from now thinning tree cover to reach rock and krummholz by the top of the chairlift. The summit cairn lies in a southeast direction, an obvious high point, above the octagonal building and beside a communications complex.

A cooling wind blows as usual. On this day it is a comfortable wind. On other days it has been powerful enough to stagger me as I move about the summit area. The open summit provides 360-degree views. I have brought a regional map to identify both neighboring 4,000-foot peaks and myriad lower peaks, ridges, lakes and ponds, and stream valleys. Sugarloaf is the highest Maine summit south of Baxter State Park. Enjoy those views!

Crocker Range

Rising between the dramatic landscape of the multi-peaked Bigelow Range and storied Sugarloaf Mountain, the Crocker Range and nearby Redington Mountain have received comparatively modest attention from the hiking public over the years. Old Speck, Saddleback and The Horn, Mt. Abraham, and Sugarloaf to the south and West Peak and Avery Peak to the north all offer 360-degree views. The Crockers and Redington, by contrast, have summits that are largely wooded.

But those who hike these peaks find that there is many a fine viewing point: fir-framed perspectives on neighboring peaks such as the Bigelow Horns but beyond as well—to Big and Little Spencer Mountains northeast of Moosehead Lake, to the Boundary Mountains north of Jackman, and even to the Camden Hills in the south. The striking cliff faces of Sugarloaf Cirque are all but hidden from view from any other vantage point but South Crocker. From North Crocker I have spotted the sun brightening snow-topped Mt. Washington—and on the same clear day enjoyed a good look at Katahdin from high on the South Crocker boulder field. Not bad for wooded summits!

A hike in this terrain offers the feel of deep-woods locales in Maine where sheer quiet prevails, and abundant animal signs tell of the passage of moose, coyote, red fox, fisher, and pine marten. You may be startled by a ruffed grouse that flies up from its feeding as you hike by, as I have been! I am drawn to the pristine nature of this range.

In 2015, some 12,046 acres of land in the region, including the two Crocker peaks, became the Crocker Mountains Unit, Maine Public Reserved Land (MPRL), thereby protecting this unspoiled landscape from development. Because this unit is an MPRL, selective timber harvesting is permitted for forest health. Proceeds fund care for this and other Maine public lands. Essentially, the new status ensures that recreational use in this, one of the more remote and undeveloped land parcels in the region, will continue.

South Crocker Mountain

Range: Crocker Range
Location: Carrabassett Valley
Elevation: 4,050 feet
Rank: 10 (tie with Mt. Abraham)
Elevation gain: 1,900 feet from Caribou Valley; 2,900 feet from Highway 27/North Crocker
Land units traversed: Crocker Mountains Unit, MPRL; Appalachian Trail Corridor; Caribou Pond Road access over private land
Fees: None
Maps: USGS Sugarloaf Mountain; Black Nubble; MATC AT Strip Map #6, Maine Highway 27 to Maine Highway 17; DeLorme Maine Atlas Map #29, 3-D

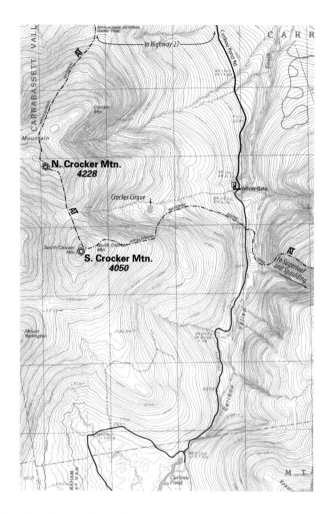

The summit of South Crocker offers exceptional views south over the valley of the South Branch of the Carrabassett River to the sharply cut Sugarloaf Cirque and to the peaks of Sugarloaf and Spaulding. The main peak of Mt. Abraham and, beyond it, Middle Peak—both distinguished by extensive high-elevation rock fields—rise beyond Spaulding. Sugarloaf Cirque is a near mirror image of Cocker Cirque below South Crocker, where an Appalachian Trail (AT) campsite is located on the cirque floor near a brook and a small mountain tarn. The valley was extensively logged in the 1980s. The forest has grown back, and the valley is now a place of quiet beauty.

As 4,000-Footer hiker numbers have grown, South Crocker has become a pivotal point of access to Redington Mountain, via a 1.3-mile (2.6-mile RT) herd path, and to North Crocker, 1.0 mile (2.0 miles RT) AT North from South Crocker summit.

- Single-peak itinerary: The shortest route to South Crocker is via the AT North, after walking 0.5 mile from the Yellow Gate trailhead on Caribou Pond Road to the junction with the AT.
- Multiple-peak itineraries:
  - From Yellow Gate trailhead to AT North, to South and North Crocker, returning to Yellow Gate. Summit South Crocker twice. Round trip. No vehicle shuttle needed. Popular with day hikers (3.1 miles OW; 6.2 miles RT).
  - From Yellow Gate and AT North to AT trailhead, Wyman Township: South Crocker, North Crocker. Point-to-point. Vehicle shuttle. Common route of backpackers leading north to Bigelow Range (8.3 miles OW).
  - Redington Mountain option: Yellow Gate to South Crocker, to Redington via herd path, and return to South Crocker; AT North to North Crocker; return AT South over South Crocker to Caribou Pond Road Yellow Gate. Cross summit of South Crocker *three times*. Round trip. No shuttle needed (9.8 miles RT) (see "Redington Mountain" chapter for herd path details).

Trails
Appalachian Trail North from Caribou Pond Road to South Crocker (Continuing to North Crocker)

Caribou Pond Road Gate (a.k.a. "Yellow Gate"), 3.9 miles south from Maine Highway 27, marks the trailhead. This gravel road is 1.0 mile north of the Sugarloaf Access Road. Make a sharp left turn near the crest of so-called Bigelow Hill. This turnoff (new green sign, 2019) is 1.6 miles south of the AT crossing of Highway 27 in Wyman Township.

The road was improved in 2018, with new ditching, bridge and culvert repair, widening of the roadway, and grading. Previously it had been prone to erosion and seasonal washouts. There are blue mile markers at miles 1, 2, and 3. The road crosses Weyerhaeuser Corporation land, as indicated by a sign 0.4 mile from Highway 27.

The Yellow Gate on Caribou Pond Road functions as the trailhead. No vehicles are allowed past this point. There is roadside space for parking but no trailhead sign and no facilities. *Do not block this gate or any other gate in the Maine mountains at any time of day in any season.* Access may be required for emergency vehicles or private owner use.

The AT crosses the Caribou Pond Road 0.5 mile beyond the gate. Watch for a roadside cairn and white paint blazes on trees and rocks. No trail sign.

- Markings: None on road past Yellow Gate; white blazes on AT.
- Maintainer: Road: private owner; AT: Maine Appalachian Trail Club (MATC).
- Distance to summit: Yellow Gate to South Crocker summit: 2.6 miles (5.2 miles RT).
- Points of interest:

  Yellow Gate trailhead, Caribou Pond Road.

  0.5 AT crosses the road. No sign. Cairns and white blazes mark the location. AT North is right (to Crocker Cirque and South Crocker); AT South is left (to South Branch Carrabassett River, Sugarloaf Cirque, Sugarloaf Mountain, Spaulding Mountain).

  1.5 Crocker Cirque campsite spur trail.

  2.6 South Crocker summit; east end of South Crocker–Redington herd path.

  Continuing AT North beyond South Crocker summit to North Crocker and Highway 27 in Wyman Township.

  3.1 Low point in col between South Crocker and North Crocker.

  3.6 North Crocker summit.

  3.9 Viewing point to north and northeast: Stratton Village; Bigelow Range peaks: Cranberry, South Horn, West Peak, Avery Peak, portion of Little Bigelow.

  4.6 Stream.

  8.8 AT trailhead, Highway 27, Wyman Township.

From the Yellow Gate, I hike on the Caribou Pond Road for 0.5 mile to the AT crossing. There is no AT sign. The crossing is discernible by the well-worn pathway on either side of the road and by white blazes on rock (left side toward Sugarloaf) and on a tree (right side toward South Crocker, 20 feet up the trail).

The trail ascends steadily through hardwoods for 1.5 miles to a spur trail leading 0.2 mile to the Crocker Cirque tent site. This is a fine location to make camp, dramatically situated at the base of the cirque. There are three tent platforms, a privy, and a single common fire ring. Water is available from a nearby brook. There is no lean-to or other hard-sided shelter.

I have used this site as a partway point to break up a longer hike in the Crocker-Redington region. Although only 1.7 miles from the Yellow Gate trailhead, the cirque camp provides opportunity for an early start on trail following an overnight stay—or a spot to spend the night after a long day of peak-bagging.

From the junction with the campsite spur, the AT climbs, with increasing steepness, up the east side of the cirque, using the South Crocker Slide for a route at a midpoint, and again near the top after a return to the woods. Views continue to open up to the east, south, and west. North Crocker commands the northern horizon.

The South Crocker summit is 2.1 miles AT North from the Caribou Pond Road. An obvious path (sign) leads southeast 100 feet to a viewpoint over Caribou Valley. Mt. Abraham's summit pokes above the ridge beyond Spaulding Mountain. Redington lies to the west. This is a remarkable view of interior mountain terrain not readily visible from any other vantage point. Quite the sight!

Hikers have choices here:

1. Hike 1.0 mile to North Crocker on the AT and return for an out-and-back hike to the Caribou Pond Road of 7.2 miles.
2. Turn around to descend to Caribou Pond Road, forgoing North Crocker.
3. Hike Redington via the herd path and return either by South Crocker or by hiking the other unmarked trail, the Caribou Valley herd path and logging road route (described in the "Redington Mountain" section), back to the Caribou Pond Road.

Hikers who choose to hike to North Crocker and return will effectively be summiting South Crocker *twice* on one trip. Those who hike to Redington and back to South Crocker will also be summiting South Crocker *twice*. Those who hike to North Crocker and back to South Crocker and then take the herd path to Redington and return to South Crocker before returning to the Caribou Pond Road will reach the summit of South Crocker *three times* on the same trip.

North Crocker Mountain

Range: Crocker Range
Location: Carrabassett Valley
Elevation: 4,228 feet
Rank: 4
Elevation gain: 2,800 feet
Land units traversed: Crocker Mountains Unit, MPRL; Appalachian Trail Corridor

Nearby supply towns: Stratton, Kingfield, Carrabassett Valley
Fees: None
Maps: USGS Sugarloaf Mountain, Black Nubble; MATC AT Strip Map #6, Maine Highway 27 to Maine Highway 17; DeLorme Maine Atlas Map #29, C-3

North Crocker Mountain is the fourth highest of the Maine 4,000-Footers. Located between better-known Sugarloaf and the Bigelow Range, it has received less attention and foot traffic over the years than these nearby mountains, but it is being redis-covered as worthy terrain as hikers look for pristine lands to explore. The township was once called Crockertown for an 1800s landowner, Thomas Crocker, but is now part of the town of Carrabassett Valley.

For North Crocker, as for South Crocker, some of the most compelling features may not be viewed from the summit. The fir waves on North Crocker, viewable from west-lying Redington Mountain, are a curious phenomenon. Gray-white bands of dying or dead fir appear on the upper slopes of high-elevation peaks. The bands result from die-off of upper branches in neighboring firs in the face of strong winds and cold temperatures. In turn, unsheltered branches on trees above also die off. Over

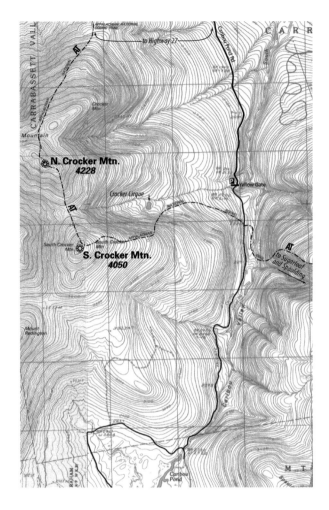

time the new growth will return to the lower-lying trees, giving the appearance—if a person returned year after year to record this phenomenon—that the bare branches are moving, in a wave, up the slope. The pattern moves, not the trees.

A viewing point just north of Redington summit provides a good look. There are glimpses from the Caribou Valley logging road route to Redington and—best with binoculars—from Spaulding Mountain. Another 4,000-Footer, North Brother in Baxter State Park, also displays fir waves.

The 5.2-mile approach via AT South from Maine Highway 27 in Wyman Township moves through an instructive progression of forest zones, transitioning from deciduous to deciduous-conifer to conifer and subalpine. The summit is essentially wooded, a curiosity given its elevation, but affords some fine views north and northeast.

- Single-peak itinerary: From the AT trailhead on Highway 27, Wyman Township, North Crocker may be climbed via the AT South, a distance of 5.2 miles (10.4 miles RT).
- Multiple-peak itineraries: Hikers commonly hike both North and South Crocker on a single day hike, as a point-to-point outing between Highway 27 and the Caribou Pond Road.
- Yellow Gate trailhead, via AT South from Wyman arranging a vehicle shuttle. The reverse of this route, starting at the Yellow Gate trailhead and ending at the AT trailhead in Wyman Township, Highway 27, is described above in the section on South Crocker.
- A three-summit option, including Redington, is to hike the herd path to Redington peak from South Crocker summit and return to South Crocker summit. (See the "Redington Mountain Range" chapter for details.)
- There is also a backpacking option, with an overnight camp at Crocker Cirque tent site.
- Trail: AT South from Highway 27 trailhead, Wyman Township.
- AT trailhead: 2.7 miles northwest of the Sugarloaf Access Road; 1.6 miles northwest of the Caribou Pond Road; 5.0 miles southeast of Stratton Village. Prominent signage on Highway 27; information kiosk; trailhead sign.
- Markers: White blazes.
- Maintainer: MATC.
- Distance to summit: 5.2 miles (10.4 miles RT).
- Distance to Caribou Pond Road Yellow Gate: 8.8 miles.
- Points of interest:
  Highway 27 AT South trailhead, Wyman Township.
  1.4 Knoll on shoulder of Stony Brook Mountain.
  2.1 Stream crossing.
  3.8 Stony Brook Mountain high point (400 feet west of summit): 3.8 miles.
  4.2 Stream crossing.
  4.9 Viewing point north toward Stratton Village and northeast to Cranberry Peak, South Horn, West Peak, Avery Peak, and a portion of Little Bigelow Mountain on the Bigelow Range.
  5.2 North Crocker summit: 4,228 feet.
  Points beyond North Crocker summit, AT South, toward South Crocker and Caribou Pond Road.
  5.8 Low point in North Crocker–South Crocker col.
  6.2 South Crocker summit: 4,050 feet; east end of South Crocker–Redington Saddle herd path to Redington Mountain.

7.3 Crocker Cirque campsite spur trail.

8.3 Caribou Pond Road.

8.8 Yellow Gate trailhead/parking area on Caribou Pond Road.

AT South

The 5.2-mile distance to the North Crocker summit provides a good opportunity to observe a fine representation of the Maine forest. Stick a tree identification guide in the pack! Here are rock maple, beech, yellow birch, white birch, and aspen (dubbed "popple" by Mainers), along with striped maple, slender striped trees with oversized leaves. In the ascent these hardwoods mix with, and then give way to, balsam fir and red spruce primarily, although there are cedars near well-watered areas, shady hemlock, and an occasional white pine as well. At a higher elevation, fir predominates, along with stunted white birch that in this ecological zone bears copper-colored bark. These high birch tend to extend laterally, rather than vertically, to minimize exposure to north winds.

Stony Brook usually flows well throughout the summer. There are seasonal run-off streams along this route, but I carry ample water because the next reliable water source southbound is at mile 7.3 from Wyman, the brook by Crocker Cirque at the base of South Crocker. The summit is rocky and wooded. Curiously, to the north, West Peak and Avery Peak, on the Bigelow Range, are at a lower elevation than North Crocker but rise above tree line!

In spite of its fir-covered high ground, North Crocker offers remarkable views from lookout points on either side of the summit. At 0.3 mile east of the top, there

MOUNTAIN MUSIC

Late one September afternoon, after ascending North Crocker from the AT trailhead at Highway 27 and summiting South Crocker, I descend toward Caribou Pond Road. What is that sound? I hear the persistent roar of a . . . waterfall? I am high on the upper edge of Crocker Cirque, well above 3,500 feet. No streams up here! Louder and louder grows the sound as I descend, and I am curious.

When I reach the spur trail to the campsite at the floor of the cirque, I have my answer: A narrow brook trickles across the trail. Crocker Cirque serves as a great sound chamber, bouncing the light rattle of this small brook back and forth across its great walls, amplifying it, raising it to the sound of a roar—sending that mountain music to the heights of South Crocker. That lifts my spirits as I near the end of a two-peak hike!

is a fine view of the Bigelow Range, over the flowage of the Carrabassett River and Stratton Brook. Below the summit to the west, an unmarked but brushed-out trail descends to remarkable slot views of the Redington Pond Range; Saddleback, Rangeley, and Mooselookmeguntic Lakes; and the peak of 3,655-foot Saddleback Junior. When the weather is favorable, the view extends to Mt. Washington!

From North Crocker, the AT swings eastward, dropping moderately and then more steadily down to the level col between the two Crocker summits. Halfway to the col I gain a view of South Crocker summit through the cut of the trail. After a nearly 500-foot elevation loss, I gain 350 feet back as I ascend to the South Crocker summit.

The AT just misses the highest point on South Crocker. A sign directs hikers to the summit viewing point, a ledge outcrop perched at the edge of the valley below. Although this sign indicates the distance to the viewing point is 50 yards, I find that distance to be about 100 feet. (I have met hikers who have walked past the viewing point, expecting a longer trek to reach it.) The views are excellent—to the south side of Sugarloaf, to Spaulding, and to the high rock fields on Abraham, which pokes above the Spaulding ridgeline.

Redington Range

The Redington name is attached to two ponds in the region, in addition to the mountain range and its main peak and a township. One pond, 90 acres, is west of Caribou Valley, in Redington Township, on property of a US Navy survival school (off-limits to visitors without authorization); the other pond, 64 acres, lies east of Sugarloaf, 0.5 mile off Highway 27, adjacent to the trail system of the Sugarloaf Outdoor Center.

These place-names are traced to Asa Redington, a former landowner of what is now Redington Township. I am attracted to the Redington area for its remoteness and undeveloped nature.

The Redington Range (a.k.a. Redington Pond Range) is distinctive when viewed from the west and north, but it is largely hidden from view from the south and east, as that perspective is blocked by Sugarloaf and the Crocker Range. A century ago, a logging railroad reached into the valleys off the north slope of the range. To the west of Redington Mountain, near Redington Pond, once stood a railroad depot. Today the area is seldom visited except by 4,000-Footer hikers and those on the AT.

Redington Mountain

Range: Redington Range (a.k.a. Redington Pond Range)
Location: Redington Township and Carrabassett Valley
Elevation: 4,010 feet
Rank: 13/14 (tied with Spaulding Mountain)
Elevation gain: 2,450 feet via South Crocker; 1,850 feet via Caribou Valley
Land units traversed: Caribou Pond Road access over private land; Crocker Mountain Unit, MPRL; Appalachian Trail Corridor to South Crocker; herd paths on private land
Fees: None

Maps: USGS Sugarloaf Mountain, Black Nubble; MATC AT Strip Map #6, Maine Highway 27 to Maine Highway 17; DeLorme Maine Atlas Map #29, 3-D
Distance to summit: By South Crocker-Redington Saddle herd path: 3.9 miles (7.8 miles RT); by Caribou Valley logging road and herd path: 5.4 miles (10.8 miles RT)
Navigation note: Redington Mountain hikers are advised to carry topographic maps and be skilled with map and compass. There is no single map that depicts the two unmaintained, commonly followed routes to the summit.

More about navigating Redington Mountain: The herd paths and old logging roads that form the approach routes to Redington are not signed or paint-blazed. Previous hikers have flagged portions of the herd paths with flagging tape, but each hiking party should have the navigation skills not to rely on such flagging. Both routes are part of a larger conglomeration of old trails and roads. Blowdowns, particularly in clusters, could block the usual routes. Due to low light, bad weather, or inattentiveness, hikers could take a wrong turn.

Caribou Pond Road and Caribou Pond are major landmarks. Hikers should establish their location on a topographic map relative to this road.

In 1998, Redington Mountain and Spaulding Mountain were added to the New England 4,000-Footer list as a result of improved elevation measurement technology. The old elevation of 3,986 feet remains on a hiker register canister located on a dead fir to the right (north) of the summit clearing.

Redington is the only Maine 4,000-Footer without a marked and maintained trail. Of the sixty-seven 4,000-Footers in New England, only one other peak, Owl's Head in the Pemigewassett Wilderness of New Hampshire, is similarly without an official trail.

Two such unofficial routes lead to the Redington summit. One that departs from the peak of South Crocker I refer to as the "South Crocker–Redington Saddle herd path." The other, which passes up through Caribou Valley, skirting Caribou Pond, I term the "Caribou Valley logging road–valley herd path."

The main peak caps the east end of the Redington Range, which forms a north–south wall rising above picturesque Caribou Valley, where Caribou Pond, with a wild trout fishery, sits at the center. Although the summit is wooded, there is a summit clearing from which there are good views of North Crocker and of the north-lying

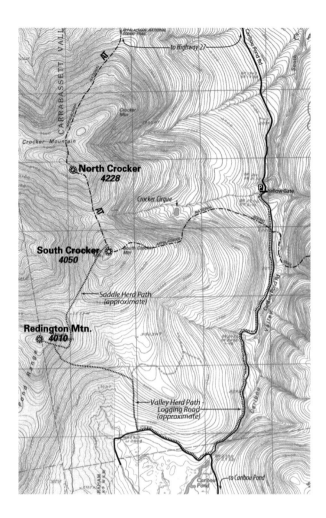

sub-4,000-foot peaks such as East Kennebago and Snow Mountain–Chain of Ponds, both on the New England Hundred Highest list. The best views may be found by stepping past a line of low fir at the west end of the clearing to an open area created by the clearing of brush.

The valley was logged through the 1980s. In the 1990s, a rough access road was built to the Redington summit to install instruments for a prospective wind turbine installation, but the project did not proceed. Today the valley and the slopes of Redington are growing back and offer visitors a renewed, pristine landscape. Birders, take note: Bicknell's thrush have been sighted on Redington.

- Single-peak itinerary: Of the two common routes, the Caribou Valley logging road–valley herd path enables a round-trip hike to Redington without passing over South Crocker.
- Multiple-peak itineraries:
    - From the Yellow Gate trailhead, a Redington hike may be combined with a South Crocker ascent via the South Crocker–Redington Saddle herd path.
    - North Crocker, 1.0 mile AT North of South Crocker, may be included in a multiple-peak hike, for a total of three 4,000-Footers in one itinerary.
    - The *return* from Redington to the Yellow Gate trailhead may be made by either (1) the South Crocker–Redington Saddle herd path to the South Crocker summit and AT North toward Caribou Pond Road or (2) the Caribou Valley logging road–valley herd path route, which meets the Caribou Pond Road at the beam bridge near Caribou Pond.
    - The valley route is longer than the saddle route but avoids a return to high elevation on South Crocker. This choice crosses moderate terrain on abandoned, grassed-over gravel roads and eventually follows the upgraded Caribou Pond Road back to the Yellow Gate. This may be a consideration in bad weather.
    - From the Highway 27 Appalachian Trail (AT) trailhead, Wyman Township: Hikers may summit North Crocker, then South Crocker, via AT South, follow the South Crocker–Redington Saddle herd path to summit Redington, and hike out to the Yellow Gate via either the saddle herd path or the Caribou Valley logging road–valley herd path route. This option would amount to a long day but is achievable for conditioned and experienced parties.
- Overnight option: An overnight at the Crocker Cirque AT campsite shortens the number of miles traveled in any one day. See "Backpacking Maine's 4,000-Footers" in the latter part of this book for details.

Trails

South Crocker–Redington Saddle Herd Path

Ascend South Crocker to reach the north terminus of this herd path, 75 feet south of the summit, on the south side of a woods clearing. This clearing and the noticeable path are to the right when approaching the signed and obvious South Crocker summit viewing point over Caribou Valley.

See South Crocker description for the route from Caribou Pond Road to summit of South Crocker.

- Trailhead: Caribou Pond Road Yellow Gate, 3.9 miles from Highway 27. See driving directions and South Crocker ascent details in the "Crocker Range" chapter.
- Markers: Route is well worn, not officially marked, with orange flagging tape along the route.
- Maintainer: Not an officially maintained trail.
- Distance to summit: Yellow Gate/Caribou Pond Road to South Crocker summit: 2.6 miles (5.2 miles RT); saddle herd path, South Crocker to Redington Mountain summit: 1.3 miles (2.6 miles RT); combined distance Yellow Gate–Redington summit: 3.9 miles (7.8 miles RT).
- Points of interest:
  Yellow Gate trailhead, Caribou Pond Road.
  0.5 AT crossing. Right for AT North.
  2.6 South Crocker summit.
  2.6 Saddle herd path north terminus.
  2.7 AT Corridor boundary (yellow blazes). Follow boundary 200 feet. Turn left. Descend.
  3.1 Sharp left turn.
  3.2 Sag and views: Redington summit ahead; North Crocker behind. See North Crocker fir waves (northeast); East Kennebago Range to northwest.
  3.3 Old logging road; turn left.
  3.4 Turn right off logging road. Route continues as herd path.
  3.7 Caribou Valley logging road–valley herd path enters from left as a woods trail. Continue ascent.
  3.9 Redington summit: 4,010 feet.
- Elevation note: Descent into the saddle from South Crocker loses 600 feet in 0.6 mile. On ascent from saddle to Redington summit, elevation gain is 570 feet. Net round-trip elevation gain is 1,140 feet over 2.6 miles.

After taking in the view over Caribou Valley and east toward Sugarloaf Cirque and the Sugarloaf-Spaulding ridgeline beyond, I step back 25 yards or so from this South Crocker summit viewing point to enter a small clearing to the west that shows signs of use as a bivouac camp. Here I locate the start of the herd path that drops from South Crocker toward the saddle and connects the east–west-lying Crocker Range with the north–south-directed Redington Range—and Redington's 4,010-foot summit.

The sky is clear. The day holds promise that I will have benefit of occasional views along the way of Redington's slopes and summit—and a good look back at the Crockers and particularly the fir waves on the heights of North Crocker. The season is high summer, mid-July. On the AT North ascent of South Crocker from the Caribou Pond Road, I have been treated to bluebead lily and bunchberry in bloom, the song of white-throated sparrow, and the rattle of the brook by Crocker Cirque.

A few steps over level ground bring me to a small wooded promontory and a quick descent. In 0.1 mile from the summit clearing, I reach the yellow-blazed AT Corridor boundary line, following it past an AT metal survey disc in the center of the trail. After 200 feet along the boundary, the route leaves the boundary line, turning 90 degrees left to descend steadily through a predominantly fir forest, with occasional steep pitches. This descent could be slow going on a wet day, but I have fine weather. Much of the elevation loss achieved, the path makes another left turn 0.5 mile from the South Crocker summit, to slab the hillside en route to the saddle.

A surprise awaits: good views, far better than I had expected. The trail emerges from dense growth at 0.6 mile to pass an open area of low hardwoods and firs, with views of the Crockers. The high ground of double-peaked East Kennebago Mountain, a New England Hundred Highest peak, rises to the northwest. A sag is next on trail, where I gain my first good look at the rounded, wooded summit of Redington, another look back at the Crocker Range, and a fine view of the fir bands on North Crocker. The footpath in this sag is boggy, not unusual in Maine's backcountry, where seeps are common, even at quite high elevations. Expect muddy conditions in the spring or following periods of rain.

Flagging and well-worn footway continue to mark the way, which ascends to an old logging road. The Redington route turns left (southeast) on this road. The turn is marked by a cairn and by brush across the road. The route continues with a brief detour around a large blowdown and returns to the road. After a road hike of 500 feet total, I turn right where logs and brush have been placed across the road and flagging has been placed, to enter the woods for the remainder of the Redington ascent.

Note: The rough logging road above continues southward to descend toward Caribou Valley. It will be joined by a lower section of the Caribou Valley herd path in about 0.3 mile. The two combined routes, logging road and herd path, subsequently descend to a broader, discontinued logging road to reach the Caribou Pond Road, 100 yards north of Caribou Pond by a rebuilt bridge over the South Branch of the Carrabassett River. Descend on Caribou Pond Road from the bridge to the Yellow Gate trailhead.

At 0.2 mile from the logging road, pass a junction with the Caribou Valley herd path, which ascends from the left (south) and shows signs of brush clearing along its route. There is a log across the trail—presumably to prevent saddle herd path hikers from making a wrong turn. There is some flagging at this corner and farther down the valley route, but I do not find it prominent at this point.

The remaining 0.2-mile ascent to the summit of Redington is moderate and clear to follow, though with some encroachment from thick trailside growth. The trail emerges from forest and turns right where an abandoned route enters from the left. I enter the fir-rimmed summit clearing in another 50 feet.

To the right of the clearing a hand-lettered sign reads "Redington 4010." Beyond this sign through the trees, a white plastic canister affixed to a dead fir contains a register. The old elevation of 3,986 feet is printed on the canister.

Beyond the clearing to the northwest there is a fine view of the Crockers and, between them, distant West Peak and Avery Peak on Bigelow. To the north lie East Kennebago and Snow Mountain–Chain of Ponds—two of the New England Hundred Highest—and the less frequented peaks and ridges that run to the Quebec border.

The clearing was cut to install measuring devices for a proposed wind farm that was never constructed. Some hardware from that testing operation may be found at the edges of the clearing. There is a compelling quiet to this setting. Not the longest views, not a maintained trail, a mountain difficult to see from afar—but a set-apart place, with its own form of beauty, now returning to its wooded cover.

On the descent, if returning to South Crocker, be attentive to continue straight (north) at the junction with the Caribou Valley logging road–valley herd path route. If your chosen descent route is through Caribou Valley, see information for that route below.

Caribou Valley Route via Logging Roads and Valley Herd Path

The Logging Road and Valley Herd Path route leads in gradual ascent to Redington Mountain. It avoids the scramble on the rocky heights above Crocker Cirque on the AT and exposure near the South Crocker summit. There is less brush encroachment than on the herd path from South Crocker summit. However, it is nearly 2 miles longer one way than the South Crocker route. Parties might consider this option if weather is poor or threatening. However, the Caribou Valley itself has its own beauty, and Caribou Pond is well worth a stop. This is an edge environment—conifers, hardwoods, the pond, some bog and run-off streams—and therefore a good locale for seeing wildlife.

Much of the route is along the Caribou Pond Road, re-graded in 2018. From the vicinity of the pond, the way is over unimproved road, some gravel, some grass and bog. In the final 0.5 mile, the way is an ascent by a narrow trail cut through the firs and undergrowth to reach the summit clearing.

- Trailhead: Yellow Gate, Caribou Pond Road, 3.9 miles from Highway 27. See driving directions under "South Crocker Mountain." Hike south on Caribou Pond Road, past the AT crossing at 0.5 mile, and into the Caribou Valley. Reach an open area, a Y-intersection, and the rebuilt bridge over the South Branch of the Carrabassett River. The improved Caribou Pond Road crosses the bridge to reach Caribou Pond in 0.1 mile. The route to Redington bears right, not crossing the bridge, and continues as gravel, in latter sections, grassy or wet, with fine views of the Redington Range. The 4,000-foot peak is to the right (north) end of the range, a rounded summit.

- Markings: No blazes; no signs. Cairns; flagging; arrow directionals formed by previous hikers using rocks and tree branches placed on the ground at points along the route.
- Maintainer: Not an officially maintained trail.
- Distance to Redington summit: Approximately 5.4 miles (10.8 miles RT).
- Points of interest (distance estimated):
  Yellow Gate trailhead, Caribou Pond Road.
  - 0.5 AT crosses the road. AT North is right (to Crocker Cirque and South Crocker). AT South is left (to South Branch Carrabassett River, Sugarloaf Cirque, Sugarloaf Mountain, Spaulding Mountain).
  - 3.0 Road forks at beam bridge. Caribou Pond lies 0.1 mile over bridge. For Redington Mountain do not cross bridge. Bear right at fork. View of Redington Peak.
  - 3.7 Road (rougher) bears slight right, ascends ridge.
  - 4.0 Before ridge crest, left turn on "old road" (cairn/arrow on ground/ flagging).
  - 4.1 Small brook runs under "old road."
  - 4.3 Left turn at junction (cairn, flagging) onto grassy pathway. (The "old road" continues straight, ascends.)
  - 4.8 Turn right at cairn, leave grassy path, and enter woods on herd path. (Trail has been clipped/flagging en route [2019].)
  - 5.1 Merge with Redington–South Crocker Saddle herd path, which enters from the right (east). Bear left.
  - 5.3 Herd path turns right at the south-end summit clearing.
  - 5.4 Redington summit: 4,010 feet. Sign on right (east) of clearing. Canister with register on fir pole in growth beyond summit sign.

On a September morning, I hike past the Yellow Gate on the Caribou Pond Road, crossing a side stream to the South Branch of the Carrabassett River, and then another, by bridges, and in 0.5 mile pass the Appalachian Trail crossing.

Red maples and sumac flutter the first red leaves of the coming fall. Ruffed grouse take flight as I make my way, startling me as they explode out of the brush, beat the air loudly, and wing away. The day is dry, bright, cool—ideal hiking weather. The wind rustles the hardwoods and subsides. The road rises gently, and the hiking is not difficult.

The first junction comes about 1.5 miles from the parking area. An old logging road diverges, ascending to the right. I remain on the Caribou Valley Road, the river—out of sight but with an audible rush—on the left. At the Y-intersection by the rebuilt bridge to Caribou Pond, I bear right. The road here becomes a varied stretch of gravel, loose rock, and sand but is clear to follow. I find an arrow at this junction, formed by sticks arranged on the ground pointing in the direction of the summit route. Such arrows have become artifacts along this way, a particular Redington tradition. I find them by junctions all along the way—some formed from branches, others of small stones or flat rocks. Such impromptu markers I ordinarily view with caution, but I have been hiking this route for over a decade and find these arrows remain undisturbed. Use your judgment!

In no more than 100 yards of hiking, I round a curve, and there, against the northwest horizon, rises the Redington Range. A rocky peak at the far southern end appears to jut higher than the wooded peak on the north end. Which is higher? My topographic map indicates that the north peak is indeed my destination. Between where I stand and the heights of this range runs a great, unbroken sweep of the

SINGS TO BEARS

The bear track, a black bear track, is as distinctive and well formed as any animal track I have ever seen—sharper in clarity than grizzly and caribou tracks I have discovered in Denali National Park, and more distinctive than the tracks of coyote and bobcat I have followed on snowshoe hikes deep in the Maine woods. I have begun a hike to Redington early in the morning following an overnight rain. The old road I am following out of Caribou Valley has many a patch of mud—nothing new for an abandoned Maine logging road.

But this section of mud is different. It holds the track—the very fresh track—of a black bear. I sniff the air. There is a distinct sour smell about—the smell of a bear, a nearby bear. A thick stand of young fir borders the route at that point. I have company, close company. Rule number one: Do not surprise a bear.

Time for a talk, followed by a song. I introduce myself to the unseen bear, as in "Hello bear. My name is Doug, and I am on a hike to Redington. Hope you are having a good day." I launch into four verses of "Waltzing Matilda" as I move on up the trail. It isn't exactly a song and dance, but I have a bit of extra energy in my step—though I am careful not to run.

I have sighted many a black bear in my hiking days. In every case, the bear, upon seeing me, ran the other way. Bears do not seem to care for the human voice. Shrieking, though, and running are not advised, lest the bear think these are signs of frightened prey.

On the return hike, the track remains in the mud, but that smell? It is gone.

Northern Forest, the old rocky roadway the one solitary opening in the swath of green.

The rubble road with pockets of sand, small nearby meadows among scattered stands of fir and pine, the bright blue sky, the dry air on this particular warm fall day—this has a Western feel, a reminder of hikes I have taken in the mountains of New Mexico and Arizona. I am not alone. Winter birds work the softwoods. Is that a rare boreal chickadee I see? Juncos, so common in the Northern Forest and often at high elevation, flit from fir to fir. On my hike today I flush out a ruffed grouse, hear the raspy call of ravens, and find in the occasional dirt patches of the old roads the tracks of fisher, coyote, even black bear.

More turns, marked by cairns, flagging, and more arrows, and I reach the end of a series of logging roads on a grassed-over twitch road, to reach the valley herd path that ascends through close fir and spruce forest to the summit. There are signs of recent brush clearing. The encroaching brush is thick along part of the route, but the way is clear enough to follow readily. I am in shorts but wear high gaiters to protect my lower legs from most of the scrapes and scratches from low spruce and fir.

I reach a junction with the South Crocker–Redington Saddle herd path, which enters from my right. The surrounding woods are thick enough that I am unable to see the summit area ahead, but the now combined herd path route is distinct. In fewer than ten minutes I reach the summit clearing.

Redington has been spoken of as having little in the way of views, but I beg to disagree! Stepping to the northern edge of the clearing and looking east, I have a fine look at North and South Crocker Mountains—and particularly those curious fir waves on the slopes of North Crocker. Beyond the two Crockers, I spot the Bigelow Range. Balancing on a summit stump, I look northwest to long, double-peaked East Kennebago Mountain. Beyond rises Snow Mountain, just under 4,000 feet, the highest peak in northern Franklin County. Clustering along the international border with Canada—more peaks. Below, still to the north, the intervale of the South Branch of the Dead River separates the High Peaks region, where I stand, from those north-lying mountains. I call that a view.

I locate the hiker logbook, packed in a canister attached to a fir tree, a few steps north of the clearing. The canister still lists the old elevation of 3,984 feet. Who hikes Redington? The log holds the names and hometowns of people from all over the United States and two recent entries by hikers from France. I add my name, noting that Redington, after my first ascent a decade earlier, was my final 4,000-foot peak in New England.

Redington is a place apart. The rewards are to cross a landscape that is reforesting to become wild and beautiful, home to many a Maine wild creature. Ascend the only 4,000-Footer in Maine with the rare distinction of no maintained trail—and enjoy the views!

Bigelow Range and Bigelow Preserve

The Bigelow Range is the northernmost of a succession of rugged ranges in the Western Mountains of Maine. Home to six major peaks—Cranberry, North Horn, South Horn, West Peak, Avery Peak, and Little Bigelow—the range offers some of the finest views in the state, from Canada to the Atlantic coast, northern New Hampshire and Vermont to Katahdin. It is flanked to the north by Flagstaff Lake, Maine's fifth largest, and to the south by the broad valley of the Carrabassett River. The Bigelow Range profile is impressive from any perspective but particularly dramatic when viewed over Flagstaff Lake from the west, north, or east.

The area is rich in history, including Native American life here over centuries, the 1775 Benedict Arnold expedition to Quebec City, and the extraordinary flooding

of the Flagstaff, Dead River, and Bigelow settlements in 1949 and 1950 following construction of the Long Falls Dam on the Dead River.

Most of the mountain range and adjacent shoreline on Flagstaff Lake is in the vast Bigelow Preserve, a 36,000-acre Maine public land that the voters of Maine authorized the state to acquire in a 1977 statewide referendum. Backcountry and lakeside campsites and access trails from the north, south, east, and west are available year-round to those seeking a Maine mountain experience with few amenities. The preserve is crossed by, or near to, the Appalachian Trail (AT), the Northern Forest Canoe Trail, the Benedict Arnold Trail, and the Maine Huts and Trails system.

The two 4,000-Footers, Avery Peak and West Peak, may be approached from the south off Highway 27 (the most popular access) or from the north, at the Round Barn area near the southeast shore of Flagstaff Lake (a more remote trailhead). Because the two summits are only 0.7 mile apart, most hikers summit both peaks on the same outing. However, it is common, and often prudent, for hikers to spend a night (or two) in the preserve because of the steepness of the terrain—and also to have ample time to experience the magnificence of this wild landscape.

Major Timothy Bigelow of the 1775 Arnold expedition is the source for the name. Reports are that he ascended to the high ground of the range for a look northward at the proposed route to Quebec.

Avery Peak

Range: Bigelow Range
Elevation: 4,090 feet
Rank: 9
Location: Bigelow Preserve, Dead River Township (T3 RS BKP WKR) (See "Hiker Talk: Terms of the Trail," appendix E, for such abbreviations.)
Elevation gain: 2,640 feet
Land units traversed: Bigelow Preserve, AT Corridor
Nearby supply towns: South side of Bigelow Range: Stratton Village, Carrabassett Valley, Kingfield; north side of Bigelow Range: North New Portland (NNP), with a diner and small grocery store; no gas. Kingfield is 7.5 miles west of NNP.
Fees: None
Maps: USGS: Stratton, The Horn, Little Bigelow; Bigelow Preserve (https://maine. gov); MATC Strip Map #5, Kennebec River to Maine Highway 27; DeLorme Maine Atlas Map #29, 3-C, 4-C, 5-C

Formerly named East Peak, Avery Peak was renamed to honor Myron Avery, major visionary and on-the-ground trailblazer for the Appalachian Trail. A plaque memorializing Avery is set on a boulder by the summit. A native of Lubec, Maine, and a US Navy attorney, he advocated tirelessly for the establishment of the AT, including its extension to Katahdin. He walked—or hiked—the talk, spending day after day in the mountains, scouting, cutting, and marking trail. Many a photograph shows him in the field, often with an axe, saw, or measuring wheel in hand. He took a particular liking to the Bigelow Range, regarding its high ground as second in Maine only to Katahdin in its rugged terrain, striking profile, and wild remoteness.

The configuration of Avery Peak is so steep that the former fire lookout at the summit did not require a tower. Rather, it sat on a 4-foot-high stone foundation. The 360-degree view from the summit includes most of the 4,000-Footers in Maine's concentration of high peaks in these Western Mountains of Maine, along with the Camden Hills on the coast of Penobscot Bay, Katahdin, and the Boundary Peaks along the international border with Canada.

Following the construction of Long Falls Dam on the Dead River and the subsequent formation of Flagstaff Lake in 1950, the south-lying Fire Warden Trail replaced the former Parsons Trail from Dead River Village as the route to the fire warden cabin in Avery Col and the fire tower on Avery Peak. The trail heads straight up the fall line from Stratton Brook Pond, gaining 2,900 feet to West Peak. Over 2,000 feet of that elevation gain occurs in the 3.9 miles above the intersection with Horns Pond Trail. Much of the upper portion consists of a series of rock steps, representing remarkable efforts by trail-building crews, considering the trailside quarrying, transport, shaping, and precision placement required for every single step. One step at a time applies on this steep trail as much as it does anywhere. I come this way often to tent at Avery Col and from there pick my way over the boulder trail to Avery summit for sunrise or sunset.

From the south side of the range, by Stratton Brook Pond, common approaches to the two 4,000-Footers are the Fire Warden Trail and the Horns Pond Trail. Both trails connect to the Appalachian Trail to complete the way to Avery and/or West Peak. Northside access is by the Safford Brook Trail from the Round Barn area near the shore of Flagstaff Lake. Note that the Round Barn no longer stands as a structure. The name applies to the site where such a barn stood until it burned down in 1950. The Safford Brook Trail meets the AT in Safford Notch. The AT is the link to the summits. It is also possible to hike the AT through the preserve, summiting Avery and West Peaks in the process. That route is lengthy and, for most hikers, involves at least one overnight stay. See "Backpacking Maine's 4,000-Footers" in the "Out of the Ordinary" section of this book.

The Bigelow Range is a true milestone for AT through-hikers. Avery Peak marks the 2,000-mile point on the trail north of the southern terminus, Springer Mountain, in Georgia. Northward, 192 miles remain to the summit of Katahdin.

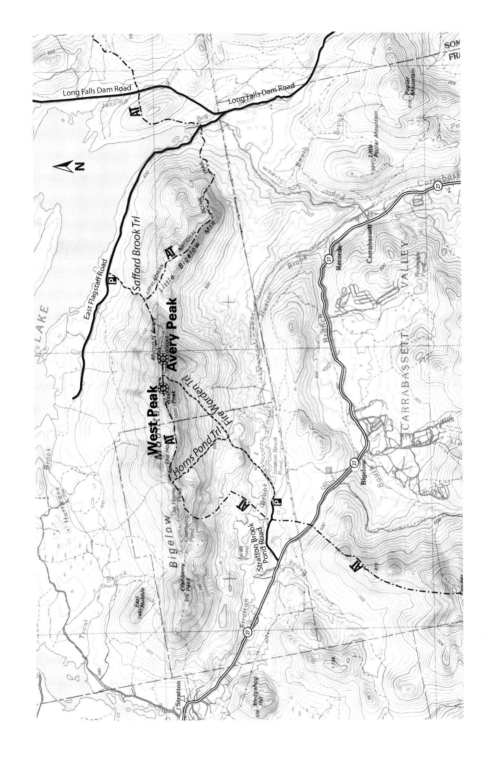

- Single-peak itinerary: Fire Warden Trail and AT North: Avery Peak may be ascended as a single-destination day hike, but with the short 0.7-mile distance between Avery Peak and West Peak, the two are commonly hiked on the same itinerary.
- Multiple-peak itineraries:
  - Fire Warden Trail and AT North and South: Ascend to the Avery Col tent site and the trail junction with the AT. From here, AT North leads 0.4 mile to Avery summit. By the AT South, West Peak summit is 0.3 mile from the col. Day hikers simply choose which to ascend first, return to the col, and summit the other peak.
  - Horns Pond Trail and AT North: A long loop hike from Stratton Brook kiosk, including a 2.8-mile ridge crest section between sub-4,000-foot South Horn (a New England Hundred Highest peak) and Avery Peak, including West Peak on the way. Descend by the Fire Warden Trail.
  - Safford Brook Trail, Round Barn to Avery Peak and West Peak: Hike from Round Barn parking area and Safford Brook trailhead to Avery via Safford Brook Trail and AT South. Continue to Avery Col and West Peak via AT South. Return to Safford Brook trailhead at Round Barn site for a loop hike or descend via Fire Warden Trail to Stratton Brook kiosk for a point-to-point itinerary.

Trails
Fire Warden Trail and Appalachian Trail North

Curiously, the Stratton Brook trailhead kiosk marking the start of the Fire Warden Trail displays no sign indicating that it is, in fact, the starting point for either the Fire Warden Trail or the Horns Pond Trail. The kiosk map does depict the parking area and the above trails. The first Fire Warden Trail sign is 1.6 miles along the trail. The first Horns Pond Trail sign is at mile 2.6.

The Stratton Brook Pond Road, 0.6 mile north of the AT crossing of Highway 27 in Wyman Township, is easy to miss. Watch on the right (north) side of Highway 27 for a blue street sign and an only slightly larger, brown Bigelow Preserve sign. The one-lane gravel road passes through a settlement of a dozen seasonal homes—used as much by skiers in winter as by summer visitors. It passes a junction with the narrow Pond Loop and enters the preserve.

After passing a bog on the right, the road reaches an unmarked AT crossing in 0.9 mile. No sign. The AT is evident due to its worn path on either side of the road and white blazes on the trees. There may be a notice or two affixed to a nearby tree, such as information about the AT hiker canoe ferry across the Kennebec River, 27 miles farther on AT North. There is (tight) space to park two or three vehicles off the road. No parking along the road, which is simply too narrow for that use.

At 1.6 miles, arrive at the Stratton Brook trailhead kiosk, where there is a Bigelow Preserve map display and notices. Park here. (The road continues for 0.4 mile to Stratton Brook but is a narrow passage, with deep mud holes and a tight turnaround space at its end.)

- Trailhead: Stratton Brook kiosk, on Stratton Brook Pond Road, 1.6 miles east of Highway 27 in Wyman Township, functions as the trailhead.
- Markers: Blue blazes.
- Maintainer: MATC.
- Distance to summit: 5.1 miles.
- Points of interest:
    Stratton Brook kiosk and parking area.
    0.4 Footbridge over Stratton Brook.
    0.5 Campsite on right. Trail turns sharp left.
    1.6 Fire Warden Trail sign.
    2.1 Horns Pond Trail junction and hiker register.
    3.5 Moose Falls campsite (left); trail to water (right).
    4.7 Avery Col; Myron H. Avery campsite (tents only; no lean-to); AT junction.
    4.8 Spring.
    5.1 Avery Peak: 4,090 feet, via AT North.
    Reverse direction to return to Avery Col and hike out or to summit West Peak.
    5.5 Avery Col and campsite.
    5.8 West Peak: 4,145 feet.

The Fire Warden Trail hike starts to the left of the Stratton Brook kiosk, on the rough continuation of the Stratton Brook Pond Road from Highway 27. In 0.4 mile, cross Stratton Brook by a planked footbridge (new in 2015). Continue straight, passing a Bigelow Preserve campsite in a high clearing to the left. Reach another campsite 0.1 mile beyond on the right (privy to left of trail). The Fire Warden Trail makes a 90-degree left turn on what continues as a level, somewhat sandy footpath. A quite worn sign at this turn reads "Bigelow Trails," with a left-pointing arrow.

As indicated above, 1.6 miles from the Stratton Brook kiosk and parking area, reach the first official trail sign confirming that this is indeed the Fire Warden Trail. The trail swings right here and at 2.6 miles reaches the junction with the Horns Pond Trail, more signage, and a hiker registration box.

My hike begins benignly along the shore of picturesque Stratton Brook Pond, where there are good views of the Crocker Range and Sugarloaf to the west and of South Horn, West Peak, and Avery Peak to the north through breaks in the trees. I

have seen ospreys and great blue herons by this pond. On other days I have hauled a canoe in and paddled upstream until thick growth and shallow depths impede further travel, discovering red-winged blackbirds in the alders and mergansers in secluded inlets.

I reach the second of two Bigelow Preserve trailside campsites, make the 90-degree turn to the left, and continue over level, sandy pathway. The surrounding transition forest is alternately spruce and occasional cedar and white pine, rock maple, yellow birch, beech, and a few red oaks. The route gains elevation, descends, rises again, moves up and over steep ledge, and arrives at the Horns Pond Trail junction and a hiker register.

Beyond this point I ascend an esker, reach a boggy area crossed by bog bridges constructed from long-sawn white cedar, and resume ascent. Shafts of sunlight reach the forest floor through openings in the canopy. Wildflowers abound on this south side of the range: Canada mayflower, bluets, and the yellow flower of bluebead lily. A pileated woodpecker rattles away.

Moose Falls tent site is next, with three tent platforms, reached by a side trail to the left, and water from Moose Brook on a separate side trail (sign for water) to the right. Beyond this point the Fire Warden Trail climbs steeply over a succession of rock staircases—gaining 1,300 feet in the 1.2 miles between this point and Avery Col. I recommend steady hiking here. Pace does not matter as much as making forward progress. On steep terrain, repeated stops and starts can be more fatiguing than a slow pace. I learned that lesson in the Sierras!

The Myron H. Avery col campsite (tents only, on platforms; privy; spring) is the highest-elevation campsite in Maine (3,818 feet) and the highest on the AT north of the Mt. Guyot shelter in the White Mountains of New Hampshire. A spring below the fire warden cabin (cabin is closed to the public) is designated on a campsite map in the col. There are other springs in the area—one 0.1 mile below Avery Col, on the Fire Warden Trail ascent, beside the trail to the west. The other is 0.2 mile AT North toward Avery Peak. The fire warden camp spring is the most reliable of the three. The others may run dry in late summer.

From the col, West Peak is a 0.3-mile, steep ascent on AT South. My destination for now is Avery Peak, 0.4 mile on AT North. The distances are short, but I have some scrambling to do on both. The Avery route crosses a boulder field in mid-trail, where foot placement matters.

I rise out of stunted firs onto a rock rubble landscape. The grade moderates. The Avery Peak sign comes into view. Soon I stand at the summit, Katahdin in view to the northeast, Mt. Washington to the southwest. A plaque honoring Myron Avery is attached to a boulder by the summit cairn.

A fire tower once stood on this summit—of unusual size and shape. So steep are the heights of Avery Peak that no tower was needed to achieve the desired view. Crews constructed a 4-foot-high rock foundation and built a cabin atop it. The cabin has been removed. The low foundation is all that remains. Imagine this assignment! All fire-tower peaks were selected for their views, of course. This one enjoyed the farthest-ranging view of all fire towers in Maine.

For an out-and-back, one-peak hike, return to the Stratton Brook kiosk by AT South to Avery Col and Fire Warden Trail (10.2 miles RT). To include West Peak in the itinerary, hike by AT South from Avery Col to that peak, ascending the rocky summit cone over a distance of 0.3 mile. To return to Stratton Brook kiosk, descend to Avery Col to meet the Fire Warden Trail. Total distance for this two-peak itinerary is 10.8 miles.

Safford Brook Trail/Appalachian Trail South

Trailhead is at the Round Barn parking area, 5.0 miles west of Long Falls Dam Road, on the East Flagstaff Road. From the village of North New Portland, drive 17.2 miles north on the Long Falls Dam Road from its intersection with Highway 16. Watch for a line of mailboxes on the right side of the road. To the left, watch for a gravel road, an East Flagstaff Road sign, and a small white-on-brown sign for Bigelow Preserve.

Map note: Some guidebooks and maps refer to this road, as it departs from Long Falls Dam Road, as Bog Brook Road, but that so-named road is now signed as a different road, one providing access to private camps by Flagstaff Lake. That Bog Brook Road diverges right (north) from East Flagstaff Road 0.8 mile from Long Falls Dam Road.

Some internet maps label the first 0.2 mile of East Flagstaff Road as Dead River Road, but that name is no longer in use for this road, instead indicating another road 8.5 miles north on the Long Falls Dam Road, near the Big Eddy campsite on the Dead River. The multiple names for roads stem from the time prior to formation of Flagstaff Lake in 1950. The Dead River Road and Bog Brook Road once served as major access routes to Dead River Township and the town of Flagstaff. Those settlements were displaced by the new lake. As indicated above, the major gravel road entering Bigelow Preserve from the Long Falls Dam Road now displays the sign "East Flagstaff Road."

Follow well-maintained East Flagstaff Road west, passing a Maine Huts and Trails intersection at 0.1 mile, the gravel Carriage Road to Carrabassett Valley on the left at 0.2 mile, and Bog Brook Road at 0.8 mile, to the right. Continue to the AT North at 0.9 mile on the right and, at 1.0 mile, to the AT South and Little Bigelow trailhead on the left. Parking for AT hikers and a primitive campsite are on the right by a gravel pit. Proceed on East Flagstaff Road to the Round Barn parking area at 5.2 miles.

Safford Brook Trail (sign) to the Bigelow Range and Avery Peak is on the left (south) side of the parking area. At the west end of this parking area, a gravel side road leads to Round Barn campsites, a privy, and a walk-in beach on Flagstaff Lake. Another Safford Brook Trail sign on the north side of the parking area points to a 0.2-mile section of the trail that leads to the shore of the lake. This short trail is a remnant of a time when the Safford Brook Trail had its northern terminus in Dead River Village. That terminal point is now underwater. Safford Brook Trail was once part of the AT prior to the reroute that now carries the AT over Little Bigelow Mountain.

- Markers: Safford Brook Trail, blue blazes; AT, white blazes.
- Maintainer: MATC.
- Distance to Avery summit: 4.5 miles (9.0 miles RT); West Peak summit: 5.2 miles (10.4 miles RT).
- Points of interest:
    Round Barn area parking/Safford Brook Trail trailhead.
    0.6 Cross Safford Brook.
    0.8 Overlook spur trail.
    2.3 Junction with AT. Safford Notch campsite (tents only; no lean-to; privy) reached by a side trail 0.1 mile on AT North.
    3.1 Spur trail left to Old Man's Head overlook (300 feet); AT South turns right to follow the height of the ridge.
    4.0 Tree line.
    4.5 Avery Peak: 4,090 feet; sign, Avery memorial plaque on boulder; foundation of former fire watch building.
    4.8 Boxed spring on trail.
    4.9 Avery Col/Fire Warden Trail to Stratton Brook kiosk.
    5.2 West Peak: 4,145 feet.
    Reverse direction to return to Round Barn trailhead (10.4 miles RT).

The route of the Safford Brook Trail follows the old Dead River Route section of the AT, in place from the 1930s until the 1950 creation of Flagstaff Lake. The views from rocky Avery Peak (formerly East Peak) extend in all directions and are among the finest to be had anywhere in Maine.

Before setting foot on the trail proper, I step 50 feet to the right of the trailhead, where a bog provides a break in the trees for a dramatic view of Avery and West Peaks. Elevation gain today! On trail I climb gradually through a transition forest of rock maples and yellow birch beside fir, spruce, cedar, and a few white pines. I cross Safford Brook by footbridge 0.7 mile above East Flagstaff Road and enjoy some trail music: a series of small cascades above the bridge rattle and clap on this day. The footpath steepens, passes a 100-foot spur to an overlook, and continues on steep grade to meet the Appalachian Trail by Safford Notch.

The Notch is well known for its house-size boulders and is worth a look. Turn left (AT North) to explore the Notch and to reach a side trail for the Safford Brook campsite (tent sites, privy). I turn right (AT South) to Avery Peak. The trail becomes very steep, with long reaches and four-point work. As the trail reaches ever higher ground, I come to a 0.1-mile side trail to a lookout point above the cliff formation of the Old Man's Head. Views over the east end of Flagstaff Lake and Little Bigelow Mountain, and well beyond to the north and east, are exceptional.

The grade lessens a bit, but only a bit, over the remaining 0.8 mile of ascent over rocky, open ground to Avery Peak, a prominent summit cairn, the fire warden lookout site, and the Myron H. Avery memorial plaque. The summit area has an extensive alpine zone, one of the finest in the Northeast—and fragile. Look down to watch hawks, and perhaps a bald eagle, ride updrafts from Flagstaff Lake below. I linger here. It is a compelling spot.

From Avery Peak the AT South descends steadily to enter krummholz, crosses a scattering of mid-trail boulders, and passes a boxed spring to reach Avery Col campsite. West Peak is straight ahead on the AT 0.3 mile. This 0.3-mile ascent from the col to the summit of West Peak is steep, with some scrambling in the final pitch.

The blue-blazed Fire Warden Trail to Stratton Brook Pond is a left turn (southwest).

Retrace steps to return to the Safford Brook trailhead and the Round Barn area.

West Peak

West Peak is the highest point on the 23-mile-long Bigelow Range. The sharp profile may remind 4,000-Footer hikers of Camel's Hump in Vermont or Mts. Liberty or Flume in New Hampshire. The open, rocky summit offers one of the finest 360-degree views available anywhere in Maine. Look northeast to Katahdin, south to peaks and hills that rim the Gulf of Maine, west to the White Mountains of New Hampshire, and north to mountains on either side of the Maine-Quebec border. Twelve of Maine's 4,000-foot peaks may be seen from the peak or approach ridge. Only Hamlin Peak and North Brother, in Baxter State Park, are out of view—this may be a factor of sheer distance. These two summits may well be viewable on a clear day with binoculars.

Nearer, look to range after range of sub-4,000-foot mountains, dozens of remote ponds and lakes—among them, Pierce Pond, Spencer Lake, Spring Lake, Chain of Ponds, and Redington Pond–Carrabassett Valley. The Dead River flows northeast out of Flagstaff Lake to join the Kennebec River at The Forks. The Carrabassett River heads south to Kingfield, then swings east to join the Kennebec near Madison. Distant Rangeley Lake drains to the southwest into the Androscoggin River, which meets the Kennebec in Merrymeeting Bay. So much of Maine within sight from this one high place!

Range: Bigelow Range	**Nearby supply towns:** Stratton Village,
Elevation: 4,150 feet	Carrabassett Valley, Kingfield
Rank: 7	**Fees:** None
Elevation gain: 2,700 feet	**Maps:** USGS: Stratton, The Horns, Little
Location: Bigelow Preserve, Dead River	Bigelow; Bigelow Preserve map (https://
Township (T3 RS BKP WKR)	maine.gov); MATC Strip Map #5, Kenne-
Land units traversed: Bigelow Preserve,	bec River to Highway 27; DeLorme Maine
AT Corridor	Atlas Map #29, 3-C, 4-C, 5-C

Lands of the Bigelow Preserve traversed here include a 36,000-acre mountain, forest, and lakeshore landscape managed by the Maine Bureau of Parks and Lands. In the 1970s, voters in Maine approved a referendum authorizing state purchase of this vast parcel—which otherwise had been slated for development of an alpine ski area. The preserve has many miles of hiking trails and over a dozen campsites. Two of the campsites are high on the range, at Horns Pond and Avery Col, and may be reached by trails that access West Peak.

Day hikers typically approach West Peak by the Fire Warden Trail or the Horns Pond Trail, from the starting point of Stratton Brook Pond, on the south side of the range. Another option is the Safford Brook Trail, with a trailhead at the Round Barn site by the south shore of Flagstaff Lake, on the north side of the range. West Peak and Avery Peak are on the Appalachian Trail. The aforementioned approach trails converge with the AT to complete a summit ascent.

The primary route described here is via the Horns Pond Trail from the Fire Warden Trail.

See previous sections on Avery Peak via Fire Warden Trail and Safford Brook Trails for details about these two other approaches.

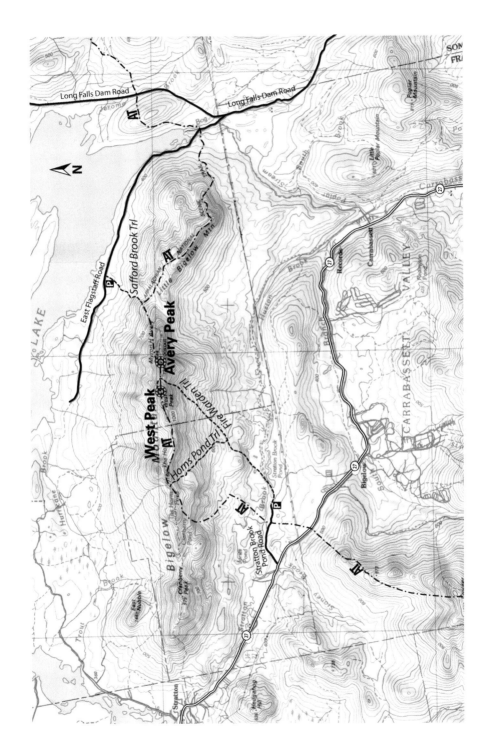

- Trails: Fire Warden Trail and AT South to West Peak (see "Avery Peak" section for details); Horns Pond Trail and AT North to West Peak.
- Trailhead: Stratton Brook kiosk, Stratton Brook Pond Road, 1.6 miles east of Highway 27, Wyman Township. The first 2.1 miles are via Fire Warden Trail. (See details for Fire Warden trailhead under "Avery Peak," above.)
- Markers: Fire Warden and Horns Pond Trails, blue blazes; AT, white blazes.
- Maintainer: MATC.
- Distance to summit: 7.4 miles.
- Points of interest:
  Stratton Brook kiosk and parking area.
  0.4 Footbridge over Stratton Brook.
  0.5 Campsite on right/90-degree left turn in trail.
  1.6 Fire Warden Trail sign.
  2.1 Horns Pond Trail and hiker register.
  4.6 AT North junction to West Peak.
  4.8 Horns Pond campsite: day-use lean-to (1); overnight lean-tos (2); tent sites.
  5.1 Spring.
  5.2 North Horn spur trail (0.2 mile to summit).
  5.3 South Horn summit: 3,805 feet (a New England One Hundred Highest peak).
  7.6 West Peak summit: 4,145 feet.
  7.9 Avery Col/Fire Warden Trail; descent to Stratton Brook kiosk.
  8.3 AT North: Avery Peak: 4,090 feet.

Horns Pond Trail

Views to the range above, ample water from a dozen trail-crossing streams, a wild-flower-filled high bog transitioning to mountain meadow, and a fishable high-elevation tarn—there is much to like about the Horns Pond Trail. An added benefit: The route spreads the 2,700-foot elevation gain to West Peak over a distance of 7.6 miles. Be prepared, though, for a 550-foot gain over the 0.4 mile above Horns Pond to the ridge crest and the sub-4,000-foot Bigelow Horns, North and South.

Horns Pond, at a 3,158-foot elevation, is the second-highest pond on the AT in Maine (after Speck Pond, near Old Speck). This is one of the most beautiful back-country campsites in Maine.

I enjoy hiking here for a night or more to fly-fish for brook trout and to enjoy sunrise, sunset, or both from The Horns. The pond is headwater for north-running Hurricane Brook, which drops northward from the Bigelow Range to empty into Flagstaff Lake.

The campsite has one lean-to specifically for day-hiker use, two Adirondack-style lean-tos for long-distance hikers, a spring, and a moldering privy. Those with time here may enjoy a hike to two viewpoints overlooking the pond. One is 0.2 mile AT South from the intersection with Horns Pond Trail; the other (signed) is off the AT North, 0.1 mile above the campsite.

A Maine Appalachian Trail Club caretaker resides at Horns Pond campsite during the summer season to oversee the site and is a fine source of information about trail conditions, wildlife, and alpine zone flora. Horns Pond is also the base of operations for an MATC Ridge runner, who is on trail daily to educate hikers and serve as a resource for questions about hiking in the region.

On the climb out of Horns Pond, now on the AT North, I pass a side trail 0.2 mile on the left to a lookout point over the pond. The pathway steepens, topping out near the spur trail north to North Horn. I make a point to make the 0.2-mile one-way hike to this peak, for this summit is one of my favorite viewpoints in these Western Mountains of Maine. Northward, the view extends up the valley of the North Branch of the Dead River to Chain of Ponds, just south of the border crossing to Canada at Woburn, Quebec. This is presumably the view that Major Timothy Bigelow sought as a member of the Arnold Expedition to Quebec in 1775.

One year I made a round-trip hike of Franklin County, the mountainous Maine county that is home to more 4,000-Footers than any other, reaching this North Horn perch on the way. From here I could see the terrain that I would cover continuing north to the border. Behind me, from South Horn, I could see much of the way I had taken from distant foothills south of Farmington. Quite the sights!

Fine as those distance views are, once on the ridge crest at the Horns, I enjoy long views up and down the Bigelow Range itself, from Cranberry Peak at the west end to the high-rising cone of West Peak. Avery Peak lies hidden behind West Peak until, of course, I reach the West Peak summit—where Avery strikes its own sharp profile. This is a fine ridge walk, but not a level one! The AT North passes over a series of high fir-covered knobs on the way, rising and falling in elevation, until the final ascent.

The all-directions view from West Peak, like that from Avery Peak, is dramatic and far reaching: Quebec, the Moosehead region peaks, coastal mountains and hills, the valley of the Carrabassett River, and the zigzag expanse of Flagstaff Lake.

One July day I meet two women on West Peak who tell me they are from Switzerland. My response: "You have some magnificent mountains in Switzerland!"

"Yes, we do," says one, "but there is nothing in Switzerland like this." With a sweep of the hand, she gestures northward to the great swath of unbroken Maine forest that stretches northward from the Bigelow Range toward Canada. She repeats, "We have nothing like this."

To reach Avery Peak from West Peak, I descend a sharp 0.3 mile on AT North to Avery Col and continue AT North beyond the col in a 0.4-mile climb to that summit. The two summits are at the shortest distance between peaks among all of Maine's 4,000-Footers, a total of only 0.7 mile—but surely a rugged 0.7 mile!

Baxter State Park

Superlatives apply, yet ultimately fall short, in describing Katahdin and the great surrounding Katahdinauguoh, the land of the highest of peaks, swift-running rivers and streams, remote wildlife-rich wetlands, and vast timber stands. Here rises the highest mountain in Maine, nearly a mile high, encircled by lake country that serves to set off the sharply rising massif all the more. The Appalachian Trail (AT) has its northern terminus here. Those who hike Katahdin via the Hunt Trail AT route encounter the greatest single elevation gain—4,000 feet—on the entire Georgia-to-Maine trail.

Ktaadn (as it may have been pronounced by the Abenaki, whose ancestral home is this remarkable terrain) is understood to mean "greatest mountain" in the fullest sense of "great." This meaning not only encompasses sheer mass and height but also invokes respect, awe, and wonder. Here great manifestations of the forces of earth, water, and sky converge. Katahdin is a place apart.

Baxter State Park (BSP) has a singular history. Most of the land that constitutes the park was purchased and subsequently donated by Percival Baxter, who served as governor of Maine from 1921 to 1925. He was an avid fisherman and outdoors person, who spent much of his time in the wilds in the Rangeley region—in sight of the Saddleback Range. Outdoor friends introduced him to the Katahdin region, and he made the preservation of Katahdinauguoh a mission in life.

Following his time in office, Baxter made the necessary land acquisitions and—stipulating that these lands were to be kept *Forever Wild*—gifted these extraordinary lands to the people of Maine to become a state park.

Baxter State Park, with its covenant commitments to *Forever Wild*, operates with a very particular set of visitor standards. I heartily recommend contacting Baxter State Park through its website and following up with a phone conversation to discuss your plans with park personnel (https://baxterstatepark.org; 207-723-5140). Do this weeks, even months, before your intended visit.

A current Baxter State Park detailed hiking map is essential. A new Baxter State Park Trail Map (2017) is for sale at park headquarters in Millinocket and at the Togue Pond Visitor Center, 0.5 mile before Togue Pond Gate at the south entrance to the park.

Fees

Day-use and camping fees vary according to the home residence of visitors—Maine or outside of Maine—and by age. Advance reservations and payment are highly recommended. Payments in the park can only be made by cash—there is no electricity to run credit card readers (see https://baxterstatepark.org).

Pointers

Over decades of visiting the park, in all seasons, summiting its peaks, hiking backcountry trails, fishing remote ponds, and backpacking to many a backcountry campsite, I

"Man is born to die, his works are short-lived. Buildings crumble, monuments decay, wealth vanishes. But Katahdin in all its glory, forever shall remain the mountain of the people of Maine."

—Percival Baxter, from a plaque at Katahdin Stream Campground, Baxter State Park

FOREVER WILD

Forever Wild was indeed a central provision of Percival Baxter's gift. The *Forever Wild* philosophy guides the park operation to this day. It is essential for visitors to grasp the practical meaning of this approach. Amenities in the park are few. The opportunity to experience some of the wildest and most rugged terrain in eastern North America and to hike and paddle and camp in remote country where the wildlife are the residents and humans are visitors is, again, extraordinary.

The wildness of the park, including the well-being of all wildlife and flora, is a priority in Baxter State Park. So is respect for the historic sacredness of this setting to Native people of the Northeast and, indeed, throughout the Americas.

have found park staff thoroughly helpful and extraordinarily courteous. Park personnel welcome visitors wholeheartedly and want you to have an enjoyable visit.

The Baxter State Park website, literature, and staff have essential information to share with visitors to this unique park and singular landscape. I offer a few selected points:

Weather events close trails or delay their opening. Seasonal storms affect availability of campsites, access to trailheads, and advisability of certain trail routes. Reservations are required for all overnight use—and are also urged for day-use parking. Parking is limited, and admittance to the park ends when parking areas are full—on some days as early as 8:00 a.m.

Park roads are gravel and narrow, with a 20-mph speed limit in most areas and 10 mph in some. Speeds above this endanger wildlife and risk vehicular accident. Sight lines are limited.

Reserve a campsite well ahead of time if planning an overnight stay. Note that campsites—tent or lean-to—have no running water, showers, laundry, and such. Water is from natural sources nearby and must be treated to be potable.

Reserve a parking space if your plans are for a day hike. Combine a party into one approach vehicle if possible, leaving other vehicles in town. If you are arriving without a parking reservation, plan to be at the gatehouse no later than 6:00 a.m. for the day's opening. There will already be a line at that time, as day visitors begin arriving well in advance of 6:00 a.m. to secure a parking space. It is not unusual on a busy summer day for all spaces to be taken by 8:00 a.m. and the gate closed to additional vehicle entrants.

Gear: The park website has recommendations and requirements for what to wear and what to have in your backpack. Pay close attention. Among other things, the park requires each member of a hiking party to have a working flashlight. For practical purposes, I carry a headlamp, with spare batteries and a spare bulb—in fact, I carry two headlamps. There are no stores or gas stations in the park.

Food and water: Each person should carry at least two quarts of water on high-elevation hikes, and the party should have means to purify water en route. I drink before I start the hike, so as to delay getting into my water stores, and make sure that I have water ready to drink in my vehicle upon my return or at my campsite if staying overnight. Eat at intervals throughout the hiking day, rather than waiting for lunch. I break every ninety minutes for water and to eat an apple or banana, peanut butter and jelly sandwich, nuts, and the like. The body is working hard!

Timing: Start all hikes early in the day, no later than first light. In late summer and fall, I begin hiking by headlamp. Hikes to the high country in Baxter State Park typically require far more time than on lower, less rugged terrain. It is not unusual for a 10- to 12-mile hike to take ten to twelve hours, including times for breaks and simply enjoying the surroundings.

Trail conditions: Expect rocky ground and, at a point on nearly every trail, some amount of bouldering, scrambling, or four-point work. This means surmounting boulders or rock slabs by using both hands and both feet. On the Hunt Trail/AT, iron rungs and footholds have been affixed to the rock to provide additional points of contact. Descent times are typically equivalent to ascent times because of the steepness of the terrain.

Pets are not allowed in the park. Most park land is wildlife sanctuary.

Terrain

Katahdin takes on a different look from every angle. From the south it rises as a great rock wall. Similarly, from the far southwest, it is yet again a massive wall, only broader and avalanche scarred. From the east it appears volcano-like, as the arc from Pamola Peak over the Knife Edge to Baxter Peak and down to the Saddle resembles the rim of a caldera—which it is not. From the north, close up, the Great Basin looks as though ripped away from the gently sloping tableland, and the rock face stands nearly sheer.

Those hiking from the west and northwest, once on the tableland, see (when the clouds lift) a great expanse of rock rubble, intermixed with the pale green of high-elevation sedge. From this angle, the peak is barely discernable, where the rock rubble ends and sky appears. Indeed, I have met hikers who were nearly at the summit but turned back before reaching it because they could not see it and supposed that it lay too distant for them to reach!

The views are extraordinary: Atlantic coastal hills; the headwaters of the Allagash and Penobscot Rivers; the unbroken terrain stretching north, west, and east to Canada; the jumble of range after range of mountains that trail off to the southwest—Gulf Hagas Range, Barren-Chairback Range, Bigelow Range, and the great swath of 4,000-foot peaks described elsewhere in this book. The short views are as captivating as the long: alpine wildflowers such as diapensia, reindeer lichen, bunchberry, and alpine azalea.

Snow has fallen on Katahdin in every month of the year. That snow accumulates in winter at depths that have kept some trails closed until late May or early June. In 2019, the Abol Trail did not open until the first week of June, and the Saddle Trail was not sufficiently free of snow to allow hiker passage until the Fourth of July week. A summit temperature of 50°F is warm. On top, the ambient temperature is often 20°F colder than at the base of the mountain. Strong northwest winds can be fierce enough to stagger hikers (I have been blown off balance to the ground while toting a hefty pack across the tableland). On the warmest of days, a weather front may pass through, sending the temperature plummeting.

Entering the Park

Two vehicle entrances, each with a gatehouse, provide access. Most commonly used is Togue Pond Gate, near the southern border of the park, 17 miles north of the town of Millinocket. This gate is the closer one to the trailheads for all three of the park's 4,000-foot peaks.

The other gate is Matagamon Gate, 27 miles west of the town of Patten in the northeast corner of the park. Because it is distant from the south-located trailheads, it is not frequently used to reach them. Park roads have a 20-mph maximum speed limit; it usually takes less time to drive from Patten to Millinocket by highway and then to Togue Pond Gate than to enter at Matagamon Gate and drive through the park.

At the gate, visitors will be asked to provide a paper copy of the camping or parking reservation. For those without parking reservations, admittance will be on a space-available basis—and then only for parking areas with space. Because this space may not be at the preferred trailhead for the planned hike, visitors should be prepared with alternate plans. A common occurrence is that the Roaring Brook parking area is full but there is a space available at Katahdin Stream. That would mean hiking Katahdin by the Hunt Trail or possibly Abol Trail—instead of from the Roaring Brook trailhead. To avoid this scenario, reserve a parking space.

Nearby Supply Towns

Millinocket is an Appalachian Trail Community especially welcoming of hikers. Here find lodging, restaurants, gear, gas, and shuttle services. The settlement at Millinocket Lake, 8.0 miles east of the park entrance, has a store, diner, lodging, and gas.

Baxter State Park is a true wilderness park. There are no retail services or gas stations in the park.

North Brother

Range: Brothers and Cross Ranges
Elevation: 4,151 feet
Rank: 6
Elevation gain: 2,950 feet by Marston Trail alone; 3,350 feet by Mt. Coe Trail, side trail to South Brother, and sections of Marston Trail
Location: Baxter State Park, Township 3 Range 10; Township 4 Range 10
Land units traversed: Baxter State Park
Nearby campgrounds (BSP): Nesowadnehunk (3 miles north); Katahdin Stream (6 miles south); Abol (8 miles south). Cabins at Kidney Pond (4 miles south); Daicey Pond (5 miles south). All accommodations are self-service, with registration required and reservations strongly advised. Overnight space fills quickly in summer and on weekends and holidays.

Fees: Day-use and camping fees apply, varying by a visitor's home residence and by age (see https://baxterstatepark.org)
Maps: USGS: Harrington Lake, Katahdin; BSP: Baxter State Park Trail Map (2017; recommended); DeLorme Maine Atlas Map #50, 4-C, 5-C
Navigation note: The Marston Trail was relocated in the 1990s away from the South Brother Slide and now passes to the west of Teardrop Pond, to ascend the east ridge of the Cross Range en route to the North Brother peak. *Some recently published maps do not reflect this new routing.* The 2017 Baxter State Park Trail Map is accurate.

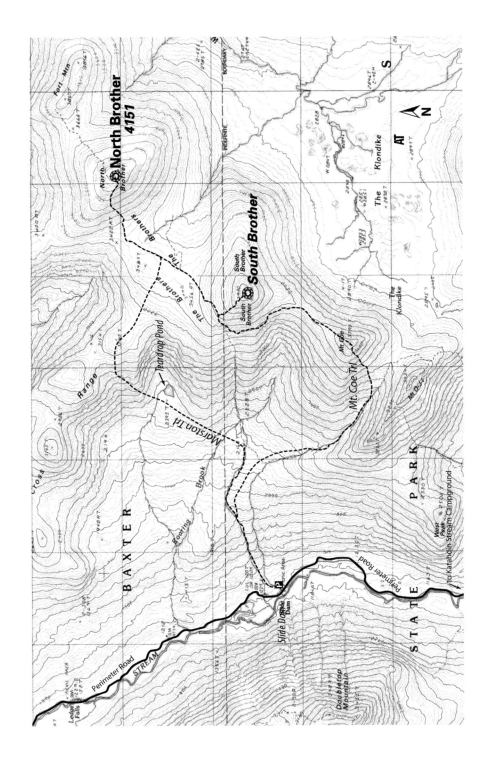

Northernmost of the Maine 4,000-Footers, North Brother rises in the interior of Baxter State Park as the highest point on the Brothers Range. So located, it offers superb views of the Katahdin Tableland, the great glacial cirque of the Northwest Basin, and the Klondike, a vast wild bog that is headwater to Wassataquoik Stream. Views extend to interior peaks: Fort, Mullen, and Wassataquoik Mountains; to the northeast-rising Traveler Range; and to nearby Doubletop Mountain. Chesuncook Lake and Chamberlain Lake lie to the west (the latter a headwater to the Allagash Wilderness Waterway).

Katahdin, when viewed from the North Brother summit, rises in a dramatic canted upsweep, unlike its appearance from any other angle. The tableland from the Hunt Trail to the summit of Katahdin is a steady diagonal slope reaching toward the peak only to end abruptly at the sharp, ragged edge of the Great Basin. Where basin meets tableland, the mountain mass appears as though torn away. This is the work of glaciers, followed by millennia of weathering by ice and snow, wind and rain, freeze and thaw. Impressive as these features are when seen up close, on a Katahdin or Hamlin ascent, they are particularly so when seen from the unique vantage point of the North Brother summit.

Two routes await the North Brother hiker. The more commonly used is the Marston Trail, which ascends from the former Slide Dam site to the summit via tiny Teardrop Pond and the Cross Range. The other begins and ends with the Marston Trail but takes a detour to climb the neighboring peaks of Mt. Coe and South Brother, both on the list of New England Hundred Highest peaks. These two summits, along with North Brother, stand in a southwest-to-northeast line, reaching toward the park's interior, each offering its own distinct view toward Katahdin and into the park's interior.

- Single-peak itinerary: North Brother is the only 4,000-Footer in this region of Baxter State Park and is reached by day hike.
- Multiple-peak itineraries: There are no trails that connect North Brother to Hamlin Peak or Katahdin. Those peaks are reached from other trailheads.

There are three peaks on the Brothers Range that qualify for the New England Hundred Highest list: Coe, South Brother, and Fort. Ascending all three, along with North Brother, amounts to an ambitious itinerary, even for well-conditioned and experienced parties. Typically, parties who seek to summit all four peaks divide the four ascents into two separate day hikes. There is no backcountry camping allowed in this region. Hikers use nearby BSP campgrounds such as Nesowadnehunk, Katahdin Stream, or Abol as a base camp.

- Trailhead: Slide Dam parking area, 13.1 miles northwest of Togue Pond entrance gate. Trailhead sign, picnic table, vault toilet, hiker register.
- Markings: Blue blazes.
- Maintainer: Baxter State Park.
- Distance to North Brother summit: 4.6 miles (9.2 miles RT).
- Points of interest:
    Slide Dam parking area/trailhead.
    1.3 Mt. Coe Trail lower junction.
    2.1 Teardrop Pond.
    2.5 Stream off Cross Range.
    3.7 Mt. Coe Trail upper junction.
    4.6 North Brother summit: 4,151 feet.

When I wish to reach the North Brother summit in the shortest amount of time, hiking the Marston Trail exclusively is my route of choice. Surely the Mt. Coe Trail loop off the Marston Trail is my preferred route when conditions are favorable, but in marginal weather, in late summer and early fall when daylight becomes limited, or if a shorter, less strenuous hike is best for my party, I choose the Marston Trail from trailhead to summit. The Marston Trail is also the shortest route to the herd path that leads to Fort Mountain, northeast of North Brother.

Mostly a forest-lined pathway, Marston Trail has limited views except for those from idyllic Teardrop Pond (mile 2.1). Pondside viewing points look across the pond—beaver activity likely—toward South Brother and its prominent slide. The slide once was part of an older Marston Trail route, now abandoned. Beyond and above the pond, the trail ascends the east end of the Cross Range where two narrow overlooks (the second, higher, one offering the better view) provide views to the valley below of Teardrop Pond, the west slopes of the Brothers Range, and OJI Mountain.

From the Slide Dam area trailhead, with a 6:00 a.m. start, I enter a deciduous forest, cross a small stream and then a larger one (both draining the Coe-OJI basin), and enter a spruce-fir forest with aging white birch. I pass the Mt. Coe Trail *lower junction* at 1.3 miles and continue straight on the Marston Trail, crossing more streams, including Slide Brook flowing in from the right, and at 2.1 miles reach the first of two openings along the west shore of Teardrop Pond. The second opening has the better view, from a short side trail to a pondside boulder. I tend to linger at such spots. The second opening offers a sitting rock for that purpose.

The trail angles northwesterly, gaining elevation steadily as it ascends the Cross Range west of North Brother. This section of trail is relatively new, replacing the former route up South Brother Slide. Water bars direct water off the trail. Rock steps limit erosion. Cedar bog bridges cross wetland—saving hikers from muddy boots and saving fragile growth from being trampled. I am impressed! This is a remote ridge for trail crews to reach. I appreciate their work—and I stop to thank them when I meet them on trail. Two streams cross the trail above Teardrop Pond; the higher one issues from a trailside spring, the last water on the trail.

At 3.7 miles from the trailhead, the Mt. Coe Trail enters on the right (south)—the Mt. Coe Trail *upper junction*. The Marston Trail proceeds across a fairly level area and ascends steeply on significantly eroded trail to reach tree line. Felsenmeer encircles the summit, and some boulder scrambling is in order. I four-point over and around the jumble and plunk down on one of the many made-for-sitting rocks by the summit sign.

The views in all directions are superb, with those of the Northwest Basin, the Klondike, the long valley of Wassataquoik Stream, the Katahdin Tableland, and the vast lake country to the north and west among the most impressive.

Fort Mountain, on the New England Hundred Highest list, lies northeast of North Brother. The route is considered a herd path and is not a maintained trail. Contact the Four-Thousand-Footer Club for directions (see amc4000footer.org).

Reverse direction for the hike out. Hiking the Mt. Coe Trail on descent is not advised because of the precipitous angle of the trail down Mt. Coe Slide and prevailing slippery conditions.

DONN FENDLER—LOST, THEN FOUND

I stand on the rocky North Brother summit with a long view of the route that young Donn Fendler, lost on Katahdin at age twelve in 1950, is thought to have taken in the first hours of what would become a nine-day ordeal. Disoriented in cold rain, whipping wind, and blinding fog, young Donn walked north, instead of his intended west, stumbled across the barren North Tableland, and thrashed his way down to the turbulent course of Wassataquoik Stream.

Nine days later, shoes destroyed by sharp rocks and pants washed away in quick water when he set them aside to wash his bramble-cut legs, he finally made his way to a spot where he was found. He had traveled overland for many a mile and made his way to the East Branch of the Penobscot River, dozens of miles to the east. A couple at a fishing camp discovered him, cared for him, and sent word to an anxious nation that he was safe. That wild and rugged terrain I look over today from North Brother is little changed from those days.

- Trailhead: Slide Dam parking area. See entry for "Marston Trail to North Brother Summit," above.
- Markings: Blue blazes.
- Maintainer: Baxter State Park.
- Distance to North Brother summit: 6.0 miles; descent via Marston Trail: 4.6 miles from North Brother; total: 10.6 miles.
- Navigation note: Hikers to North Brother via Mt. Coe and South Brother are advised to descend North Brother entirely by the Marston Trail (4.6 miles) directly to the Slide Dam trailhead. The Mt. Coe Trail in ascent negotiates steep and slippery rock slabs on the Mt. Coe Slide. Descending the slide is difficult, even dangerous.
- Points of interest:
  Slide Dam trailhead by Marston Trail.
  1.3 Mt. Coe Trail lower junction.
  1.5 Base of Mt. Coe Slide.
  2.7 Junction with the Mt. OJI Link Trail (to right of slide).
  3.1 Top of slide.
  3.3 Mt. Coe summit.
  4.5 South Brother spur trail to summit; 0.3 mile to summit (0.6 mile RT).
  5.1 Marston Trail upper junction.
  6.0 North Brother summit: 4,151 feet.

I consider the longer Mt. Coe route one of the truly outstanding ridge traverses in the Northeast. It offers many more views than the Marston route alone, including extensive looks into the Klondike, ever-changing perspectives on Baxter Peak and the surrounding high ground, and multiple opportunities to see the fir-wave phenomenon on both North and South Brother. Hikers choosing this route may summit at least three New England Hundred Highest peaks (Coe and the two Brothers) in one hike.

At 6:30 a.m. I sign the hiker register at Slide Dam parking area, after camping overnight at Abol Campground, 8 miles south on the Perimeter Road. I look forward to a fine day on the Brothers Range, with clear skies, but surely a long day: three peaks, a 3,350-foot elevation gain, a steep slide to negotiate, 10.6 miles of trail. A few steps into the woods, I cross a broad stream by rock step, the thin rush of the water the only sound at this quiet hour.

It is a short, mostly level walk to the Mt. Coe Trail junction at mile 1.3 on the Marston Trail, marked by a trail sign. The trail soon meets Slide Brook, with its mini-cataracts, which it follows, with occasional rock-step crossing on my part, to the base of the Mt. Coe Slide. During high-water periods, Slide Brook may be difficult to ford. Massive scree banks along and above the south side of the brook, formed by run-out from the slide, are testimony to the tremendous forces of meltwater during spring runoff and at any time of year following strong storms.

The route leaves much of the scree behind to ascend the steep and wet rock slabs, many moss covered, of Mt. Coe Slide. The blazed and cairn-marked route moves back and forth across the slide to take advantage of occasional sections of scree patches and dry rock. This is not easy going. I consider each foot placement with care, and step by step, here and there, inch by inch, I progress upward.

The Mt. OJI Link Trail diverges on the far right at a point approximately 0.2 mile up the open slide. The trail sign may be difficult to see as it is close to woods across the slide from my vantage point and is shaded this early in the day. The OJI Link Trail reaches the OJI ridge in 0.5 mile.

Higher on the slide, the route stays left. I watch carefully for cairns. The trail enters the scrub 0.2 mile short of the open Mt. Coe summit, which offers outstanding views of the Katahdin massif, the Owl promontory west of the Hunt Trail on Katahdin, and the southern extent of the Klondike. I linger here, taking the first of many long looks into the park's wild interior that I will enjoy this day.

From the summit, I hike north along narrow summit ledge—next stop South Brother, which stands impressively ahead across a deep intervening saddle. There is a side trail to the left, just beyond the summit, which leads 30 feet to end at a small clearing amid the krummholz. This spot offers a windbreak for blustery days. The main trail drops steeply down off the ledge to descend to the saddle, then levels, holding to contour for much of the way to the South Brother spur trail (sign).

An old Mt. Coe Trail sign remains in the firs just before the spur, a remnant of the time when the Marston Trail ascended the South Brother Slide. That route was discontinued in the 1990s, and the route is obliterated. That sign captures my attention—a trail sign completely surrounded by trees and undergrowth, no indication of a connecting trail anywhere. This spot is a long hike from the road. I assume it was not a trail crew priority to dismantle the 18 × 18–inch square sign and haul it off, but no one wanted to litter the mountains by tossing it into brush either. (I check my map to confirm my location.)

The 0.3-mile spur hike (0.6 mile RT) to South Brother is well worth the effort. At a halfway point the route reaches a series of high boulders, requiring some scrambling, which continues nearly to the open summit. The views complement those from Coe, offering a different angle of view to Katahdin, the Klondike, and the interior reaches of the park.

A sighting! Far to the east, across the full width of the park, I spy a promontory above the valley of Wassataquoik Stream. Morning sun hits summit ledge on that high ground, brightening the summit. That point is called "The Lookout," a low peak, elevation 1,950 feet, at the western edge of Katahdin Woods and Waters National Monument. Four months ago, on a three-day winter trip to the monument—traveling mostly on skis and pulling pulk sleds—a companion and I changed to snowshoes at the base of The Lookout and made the ascent. On that day, sun filled like this one (though far colder), I peered into the interior of the park from the east, beheld the unique view of Katahdin from that rare angle, and enjoyed a good look at the heights of the Brothers Range where now I stand.

On today's outing, I descend the South Brother spur back to the Mt. Coe Trail and turn right (north). The pathway follows fairly level ground to the junction with the Marston Trail. From here to the open summit of North Brother is 0.8 mile.

Until the trail emerges above tree line, the way is heavily wooded with no views— to a hiker's advantage in windy conditions.

See "Marston Trail to North Brother Summit," above, for my observations of the high ground on North Brother.

Hamlin Peak

Hamlin is an impressive mountain, looming above Chimney Pond, North Basin, the South Branch of Wassataquoik Stream, the Turner and Traveler Ranges, and the wild and rocky North Tableland. Views of Katahdin and the Knife Edge, the Cathedrals along Cathedral Trail, the great couloir of the Chimney, and the sharp, glacier-carved rock face of the Great Basin are striking. Arguably, Hamlin provides the best view of Katahdin in all of Baxter State Park. If this 4,756-foot peak rose somewhere else in Maine or elsewhere in New England, it surely would command great notice on its own merit.

Range: Katahdin massif
Location: Baxter State Park
Elevation: 4,756 feet
Rank: 2
Elevation gain: 3,700 feet (varies by route)
Location: Mt. Katahdin Township (Township 3 Range 9)

Fee: Day-use and camping fees apply, varying by state of residence (see https://baxterstatepark.org)
Maps: Baxter State Park map (2017; recommended); USGS: Katahdin; DeLorme Maine Atlas Map 50, 4-C, 5-C

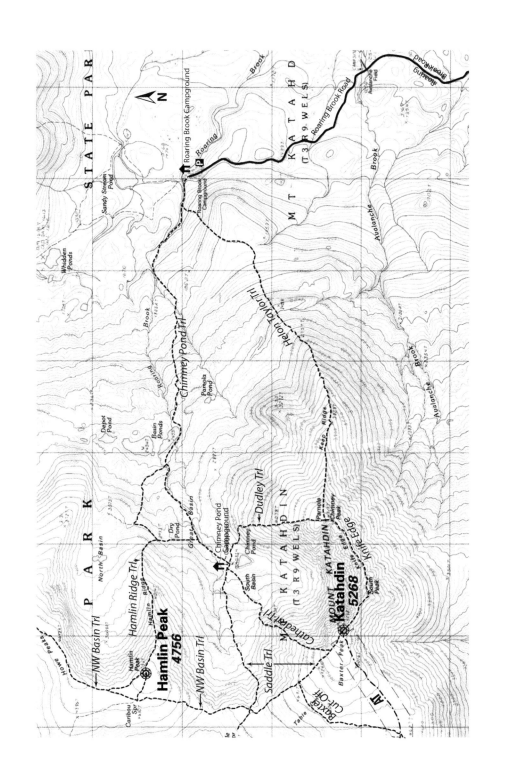

Among the sixty-seven New England 4,000-Footers, Hamlin is all but tied for twelfth place with New Hampshire's North Twin, the two separated by only 1 meter of elevation. Hamlin is higher than such iconic peaks as Vermont's Mt. Mansfield and Camel's Hump, and New Hampshire's Mts. Carrigain, Garfield, and Liberty, Middle and South Carter, and Wildcat—all far better known to the hiking community.

Hamlin Peak's lack of notoriety surely results from being situated only 2 raven-fly miles from one of the most legendary peaks in the world: Katahdin. It once seemed that Hamlin was forever destined to stand in the shadow of its famous neighbor, both literally and figuratively. However, the Four-Thousand-Footer Club, with its proclaimed goal of exploring lesser-known higher peaks of New England, has drawn fresh attention to Hamlin, with its singular views toward Katahdin and into the Great Basin and the other glacial cirques northeast of Katahdin.

The names Hamlin Peak and Hamlin Ridge are derived from Charles E. Hamlin, who was a professor at Colby College and later at Harvard College. Hamlin made many trips to the Katahdin area, beginning in 1869, to study the geology of the region. He advocated creating public access to this highly remote region, including overnight lodging. Professor Hamlin envisioned, a century and a half ago, that days spent among these peaks (one of which would eventually bear his name) would be of great benefit to the human spirit.

- Single-peak itinerary: Although Hamlin may be summited along with Katahdin in a single-day hike, a good number of hikers undertake a hike of Hamlin by itself. This may be the choice in consideration of weather, hours of available daylight, or hiker interest in allocating ample time to explore the felsenmeer (boulder field) and alpine flora on Hamlin Ridge. Hiking Hamlin by itself may provide time for a hiking party to explore the nearby North Tableland, uniquely wild and beautiful, almost entirely above tree line, and lightly visited.

- Some parties may have summited Katahdin by itself on another occasion or plan to do so.

- There are many itinerary options for Katahdin, some requiring ten hours or more, causing hikers not to have time, or the inclination, to include Hamlin. Others may wish to conserve their energy by hiking one day, one peak.

- The above considerations could apply to hikes to most, if not all, of Maine's 4,000-Footers. Each party, in its planning, might include these factors when deciding how extensive an itinerary to undertake for any of these peaks. "Hike your own hike" is a well-known trail mantra. What matters is not how fast or slow one party is in comparison to another. What matters is for the members of a given party to have a quality experience in the mountains, returning safely to the starting point.

- Both an out-and-back option (direct to the peak from Roaring Brook Campground) and a loop option (incorporating Chimney Pond and the Saddle Slide) are available to summit Hamlin Peak.
- Multiple-peak itinerary: When combined with Katahdin, Hamlin Peak may be summited in a great ridge crest loop that includes the Knife Edge, Katahdin summit, the Saddle and Northwest Basin Trails, and the Hamlin Ridge Trail. This loop begins and ends at Roaring Brook Campground. Hikers may proceed in either direction. (See "Katahdin" section below for details.)

Trails
Roaring Brook to Hamlin Peak (Out-and-Back Hike)

- Shortest route to and from Hamlin Peak.
- Trails: Chimney Pond Trail 2.1 miles to North Basin cutoff, 0.7 mile into North Basin, 0.2 mile south to Hamlin Ridge Trail, 1.3 miles west to summit.
- Trailhead: Roaring Brook Campground.
- Markers: All trails listed—blue blazes.
- Maintainer: BSP.
- Distance to summit: 4.5 miles (9.0 miles RT).
- Points of interest:
    Chimney Pond Trail.
    Roaring Brook Campground ranger station/trailhead (all hikers sign register on ranger station porch).
    0.1 Pass junction with Helon Taylor Trail to Pamola Peak and Knife Edge.
    1.0 Pamola Brook.
    1.9 Basin Pond: Side trail to shore view of Hamlin Peak and the Howe Peaks.
    2.1 Junction with North Basin Cutoff. Turn right.
    2.8 Junction with North Basin Trail. Turn left.
    3.0 Junction with Hamlin Ridge Trail. Turn right.
    4.5 Hamlin Peak: 4,756 feet.
    Reverse direction to return to Roaring Brook Campground.

This most direct route to Hamlin Peak uses two short connecting trails—the North Basin Cutoff and North Basin Trail—to bypass Chimney Pond and avoids backtracking from the pond to reach the Hamlin Ridge Trail. When hiked as an out-and-back itinerary, it provides the shortest total distance to reach the summit and return to Roaring Brook Campground and trailhead.

I typically camp overnight at Roaring Brook Campground the night before an ascent in order to gain an early start. The Togue Pond Gate, the southern vehicle entrance to the park, ordinarily opens in summer at 6:00 a.m. A long line of hiker vehicles usually waits to be processed, even at that early hour. For me, sometime between 5:00 and 6:00 a.m. is my preferred hour to start a hike; I want to make maximum use of the daylight hours and have ample light at the end of the day for my descent. Before the first vehicle of the day from Togue Pond Gate reaches the parking area at Roaring Brook, I am a mile or more up the trail.

Wearing my headlamp, I sign the hiker register on the porch of the ranger station and head out. Chimney Pond Trail is but a few steps away, north of the ranger station, where a footbridge crosses Roaring Brook for north-lying trails and the Chimney Pond route is a left turn (west). The brook lives up to its name, with a clear-throated roar so loud as to drown out conversation. I often step to the center of the bridge for a moment to listen—like turning up the sound on speakers full blast—watch the clear waters roil, smell the sweet coolness that hangs over mountain streams like this one.

Back from the bridge and on trail, I keep a steady pace over a gently rising and fairly clear footpath. The way steepens; rocks and small boulders punctuate the footpath—this is the character of Chimney Pond Trail over much of its length—except for a section of boardwalk and a wide planked bridge, constructed for BSP emergency snowmobile access. Basin Ponds are a marker of progress. I take the short side trail to the shore, where Hamlin Peak rises front and center, a fine view that shows off this second-highest mountain in Maine, in due relief. The Howe Peaks, to the right (north) of Hamlin, have a prominence here seen from nowhere else. In winter the trail passes across the frozen surface of the ponds. In summer the route skirts the south end of the ponds as it continues to climb westward.

The North Basin Cutoff, combined with the North Basin Trail, is a shortcut to the Hamlin Ridge Trail. Otherwise hikers would ascend to Chimney Pond and backtrack. *Note:* For those who wish to go directly to Chimney Pond first—perhaps with a lean-to or bunkhouse reservation for an overnight stay, or simply for a good look at the pond—instead of turning onto the North Basin Cutoff, continue on Chimney Pond Trail for 0.9 mile.

At the junction with the North Basin Trail, I turn left (south)—that is, unless I have the North Basin in my itinerary. For a fine look into this basin between Hamlin and the Howe Peaks, a look back toward the Great Basin, and a view down toward Sandy Stream Pond, Whitten Pond, and up to the east-lying Turner Range, I make the 0.2 mile (0.4 mile RT) side trip to Blueberry Knoll, a day-use spot at the edge of North Basin. The view to Hamlin and the Howe Peaks above is impressive. Massive rock-strewn slopes drop down to the basin floor. Quite the sight.

Returning to the North Basin Trail in the direction of Hamlin, I reach the Hamlin Ridge Trail in 0.2 mile and turn right (west) to begin a 1.5-mile steady and steep ascent to the peak. There are a few long reaches to negotiate rock slabs. This is typical high-ground ascent terrain in Baxter State Park, where the footpath moves up over boulders, ledge, and scree into an alpine zone. Every bit of ascent brings new views into the North Basin and Great Basin on either side.

The very top, after all that effort, is unassuming—one rounded section of rock rubble marginally higher than the surrounding felsenmeer. A sign planted in a low cairn marks the summit. It is the view over the tableland that grabs my attention. Acres and acres of rock lie to the north, west, and south. I am tempted to use the term "moonscape," but the alpine environment here is full of life: sedge, diapensia, sandwort, mountain cranberry, krummholz.

For an out-and-back hike, I reverse direction for the descent, long views before me.

Roaring Brook to Hamlin Peak with Descent via Saddle Trail and Chimney Pond

- Loop hike (shortest loop).
- Trailhead: Roaring Brook Campground.
- Trails: Follow ascent route to Hamlin Peak described in the Hamlin out-and-back entry above. From Hamlin summit, head west on Hamlin Peak Cutoff to junction with Northwest Basin Trail near Caribou Spring. Take Northwest Basin Trail to the Saddle Trail. Descend Saddle Trail to Chimney Pond, then Chimney Pond Trail to Roaring Brook.
- Markers: Blue blazes.
- Maintainer: BSP.
- Distance to summit: 4.5 miles (loop from/to Roaring Brook: 10.1 miles).
- Points of interest:
    Continuing hike from Roaring Brook to Hamlin Peak (cumulative miles from Roaring Brook)
    4.5 Hamlin Peak; junction with Hamlin Peak Cutoff.
    4.7 Junction with Northwest Basin Trail. Turn left (south).
    4.7 Spur to Caribou Spring straight ahead, 50 yards (west); worn pathway, blue blazes.
    5.8 Junction with Saddle Trail; head of Saddle Slide. Turn left (east) to descend.
    7.2 Chimney Pond Campground; junction with Chimney Pond Trail.
    10.5 Roaring Brook Campground.

This loop summits Hamlin early in the hike, provides time to spend at the edge of the intriguing high North Tableland, and offers continuing looks at Katahdin and the Great Basin from changing viewpoints. This option permits hikers to visit Chimney Pond, center of the Great Basin, at the latter part of a Hamlin Peak hike.

A HEADLAMP IN EVERY PACK

Baxter State Park requires that each hiker carry a flashlight, regardless of whether the party expects to be out after dark. The time required to hike Baxter State Park trails usually exceeds that of most other trails in eastern North America. Many parties find themselves still on trail at sunset.

A headlamp is the most practical source of light because hikers need to have their hands free and the trail illuminated ahead. I carry a spare set of batteries. In case of a mishap, whether to me or someone in my party, I may need light for an entire overnight. I carry a spare headlamp in case mine, or that of a member of my hiking party, fails to work.

Chimney Pond is one of the park's truly extraordinary natural features. Massive cliff walls, cut by couloirs and sharp buttress ridges, soar upward to Katahdin and the Knife Edge. Snowfields, some lasting into June and even July, feed this clear high pond. Come here to behold the reflection of Katahdin's high ground on the surface of the water. By hiking Hamlin before reaching Chimney Pond, once at the pond, parties may better determine how much time they may spend there, without the pressure of a yet-to-be-fulfilled summit hike.

From Hamlin Peak, I hike west on the Hamlin Peak Cutoff in gradual descent to reach the Northwest Basin Trail. Straight across this junction a spur trail leads 50 yards to Caribou Spring. Although it is high on the tableland and subject to running low in late summer, I have not yet found it to be dry. The water is so fresh and cold that I make a stop whether I need water or not. I purify it, of course—it is a source for animals of the tableland as well as for people.

In the direction of the Saddle Trail and Saddle Slide, as I descend to this great col—The Saddle—between Hamlin and Katahdin, I have a dramatic view of the southern sweep of the tableland up to the peak of Katahdin: the Knife Edge angling to the east of the Katahdin summit in a serrated arc reaching, right to left (west to east), from Baxter Peak to South Peak, over a series of unnamed rocky knobs, and on to Cathedral and Pamola Peaks.

The Saddle Slide descent is a one-step-at-a-time affair, over scree, and with some downward scrambling. No rush; plant one foot, and then the other. Trekking poles provide stability. Pause for the view! At Chimney Pond I take a good break by the pond, when the weather is favorable, or back under the sizable day-use shelter in the center of the campground when the winds blow and the temperature chills.

I descend back to Roaring Brook, keeping my eyes open for moose. A number of times I have seen moose, including a great bull, trailside just below the campground on the Chimney Pond Trail. Eventually the roar of the brook welcomes me back to Roaring Brook Campground.

Katahdin

Range: Katahdin massif
Location: Baxter State Park; Mt. Katahdin Township (Township 3 Range 9 West of Eastern Line of State)
Elevation: 5,268 feet
Rank: 1
Elevation gain: 4,000 feet
Fee: Day-use and camping fees apply, varying by residence and age (see https://baxterstatepark.org)
Maps: USGS: Katahdin; Baxter State Park trail map (2017); DeLorme Maine Atlas Maps #50, 5-C, 5-D; #51, 1-C, 1-D
Itineraries: Nine trails approach the summit of Katahdin from three trailheads:

From the east, Roaring Brook Campground is the trailhead for two major approaches: Chimney Pond Trail and Helon Taylor Trail. Chimney Pond Trail connects to four ascending trails near the Great Basin: Dudley, Cathedral, Saddle, and Hamlin Ridge. Helon Taylor Trail meets the Knife Edge Trail at Pamola Peak.

Two west-lying trails are Hunt Trail, which is the route of the AT, and Abol Trail, which meets Hunt Trail at Thoreau Spring on the tableland.

From the north, two lesser-traveled routes are the North Peaks Trail and the Northwest Basin Trail. Most hikers overnight at the Russell Pond or Wassataquoik Stream lean-tos, in the interior of the park, before such a hike. Roaring Brook Campground has the nearest parking for the approach hike to Russell Pond.

Eastern Approaches

Roaring Brook is the most popular trailhead in Baxter State Park, serving the large network of trails east of Katahdin and interior sections of the park in the Russell Pond–Wassataquoik Stream area. It is also the trailhead for hikes to South Turner Mountain and to Sandy Stream Pond (the latter being a good location to spot moose).

Most common hikes to ascend to the Katahdin Tableland and from there to reach the summit:

- Chimney Pond Trail to Saddle Trail
- Helon Taylor Trail to Knife Edge Trail
- Chimney Pond Trail to Hamlin Ridge Trail

Two other routes provide options from Chimney Pond Campground: Cathedral Trail and Dudley Trail.

- Trails: Chimney Pond Trail to Saddle Trail to summit. Descend by reverse direction or by Knife Edge and Helon Taylor Trail.
- Trailhead: Roaring Brook Campground.
- Markings: Blue blazes.

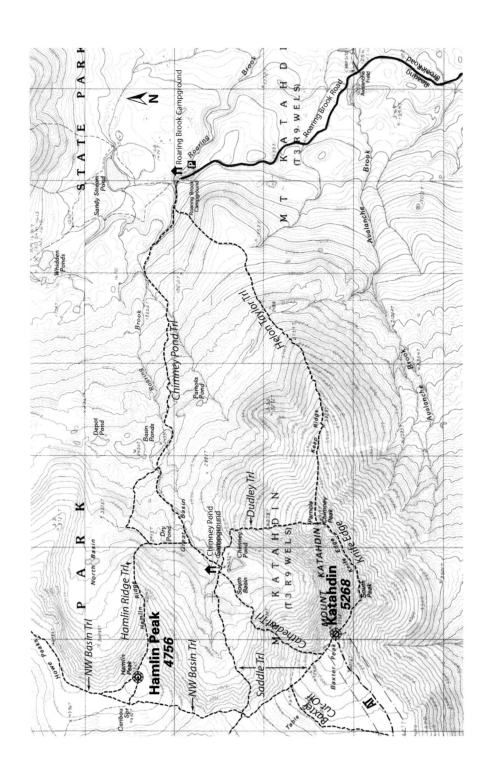

- Maintainer: BSP.
- Distance to summit: 5.0 miles (10.0 miles RT).
- Features: Chimney Pond with Great Basin views; Saddle Trail views south to Knife Edge and west to Hamlin Ridge; tableland hike to summit. Saddle Slide is steep in upper sections, with scree. This is the most popular route to the summit, with the least scrambling and four-point work.
- Points of interest:
    Roaring Brook Campground ranger station/trailhead (sign in on hiker register).
    0.1 Pass junction with Helon Taylor Trail to Pamola Peak and Knife Edge.
    1.9 Basin ponds.
    3.0 Chimney Pond Campground; junction with Saddle Trail.
    4.4 Head of Saddle Slide; junction with Northwest Basin Trail. Saddle Trail turns 90 degrees left (south).
    4.5 Cathedral Trail Cutoff.
    4.8 Cathedral Trail junction.
    Katahdin summit: 5,268 feet.
    For out-and-back hike, reverse direction (10.0 miles RT).

Once, on the summit of Katahdin, I was asked by a hiker what is the easiest trail on the mountain. I paused, ran the nine different approach trails through my memory, and replied, "There isn't an easiest trail." I was not seeking to be difficult. The reality is that all approach trails are steep and require some combined hands and feet (a.k.a. four-point) work. Of all the approaches, the Saddle Trail is often considered the least difficult, but that assessment is relative. The upper reaches of the Saddle Slide require full attention to foot placement and the capacity to proceed where there is significant exposure. (Exposure, in mountaineering terms, refers to steepness and the visible drop-off of the slope.)

Chimney Pond Trail descriptions may be found above under "Hamlin Peak." I pick up the description of this route at Chimney Pond Campground, trailhead for the Saddle Trail. For over a century this has been a popular route for a Katahdin ascent. The trail moves upward steadily through fir and spruce forest, crosses Saddle Stream, and then steepens. Expect some long reaches in a section of boulders and rock slabs, still amid forest growth that tends toward krummholz. In the final 0.2 mile before the tableland, there is considerable scree to negotiate. It is but a few feet from the top of the slide at the edge of the tableland and the junction with the Northwest Basin Trail. Here the Saddle Trail turns left (south) toward the summit.

Considerable rock-step construction and ample paint blazing make the route usually clear to follow and keeps hikers away from the delicate alpine flora on either side of the trail. There have been extensive efforts over the past two decades to educate hikers about the fragility of plants in the alpine zone. Kindly protect alpine plants. Please stay on the trail.

On the way, the Saddle Trail passes a junction with the Cathedral Trail Cutoff, 0.6 mile before the summit, leading from the Cathedral Trail, which ascends Katahdin from Chimney Pond. A junction with the Cathedral Trail itself follows in another 0.4 mile. The summit stands 0.2 mile above this junction.

The rounded slope of the tableland and the low profile of the summit when approached by the Saddle Trail may cause hikers to not recognize how near they are to the summit in this final 0.2 mile. The large summit sign appears first, typically with a gathering of hikers nearby. An 8-foot cairn stands a few feet to the left (southeast) of the sign. The Saddle Trail meets the summit at a point only a few steps from the precipitous edge of the Great Basin. The Knife Edge, with its undulating line of bare rock, arcs to the east. To the west and northwest, the vast tableland slopes away, endless rock and sedge. The Brothers Range rises to the northwest, North Brother the highest peak to the right. The vast lake country—Chesuncook, Chamberlain, and Eagle Lakes—lies farther still in that direction.

The out-and-back hike reverses direction here, via the Saddle Trail and Chimney Pond Trail. For a loop hike, returning to Roaring Brook via Knife Edge and Helon Taylor Trails, continue the hike over the Knife Edge Trail, 1.1 miles to Pamola Peak and the Helon Taylor Trail junction.

South Peak, barely 28 feet lower than Katahdin in elevation, is the first peak on Knife Edge, followed by a series of short descents and ascents over rocky knobs on the route. Beyond South Peak there are places where the rock footway narrows to 2 to 3 feet in width, with significant exposure on either side. Western hikers may be reminded of the narrow way on Glen Pass and Forester Pass in the Sierras or perhaps the long view down from Eagle Creek Canyon or Kendal Katwalk on the Pacific Crest Trail.

Trails
Descent via the Knife Edge

To descend via the Knife Edge, from Katahdin's summit take the Knife Edge Trail to Pamola Peak and then the Helon Taylor Trail to the Roaring Brook Campground.

Legendary and spectacular, Knife Edge is an arête, formed by glacial activity on both sides of a ridge. In the eastward direction, the narrow trail summits South Peak (5,240 feet), Chimney Peak (4,900 feet), Pamola Peak (4,919 feet), and intervening promontories. Views are into the Great Basin to the north, over the south-lying lake and hill country toward the Atlantic coast. Helon Taylor Trail continues the descent with eastward views over Katahdin Lake and the East Branch of the Penobscot River.

- Points of interest:
  From Katahdin summit, cumulative miles from Roaring Brook start
  5.3 South Peak.
  6.0 Chimney Peak.
  6.1 Pamola Peak; junction with Helon Taylor Trail and Dudley Trail.
  9.7 Roaring Brook Campground and ranger station.

LIFE ON THE EDGE

Over the decades some Katahdin hikers, weary or unsettled by the Knife Edge effort, or apprehensive about changing weather, have attempted to go off-trail on the Knife Edge, seeking an alternate way down. *There is no safe alternate way. Never attempt a shortcut off the Knife Edge. Do not attempt to cross the Knife Edge when members of the party are unduly fatigued or poor weather is present or imminent.*

The col between Chimney Peak and Pamola requires care in descent and ascent, with long reaches. I use all fours here. At Pamola Peak, I stop for a good look back at the Knife Edge and the Katahdin summit and down into the Great Basin. Once I step away to descend the Helon Taylor Trail, those astounding views will be out of sight.

On the final 3.6 miles to Roaring Brook Campground, I remind my party to stop for water and food breaks. The body needs sustenance on the descent. Remember to sign out at the hiker register on the ranger station porch!

Helon Taylor to Knife Edge: For Descent by Saddle Trail or Chimney Pond Trail (or via Hamlin Peak)

- Trailhead: Roaring Brook Campground.
  - Clockwise route ascends Helon Taylor Trail to Pamola Peak; Knife Edge Trail to Katahdin (Baxter Peak). Descend Saddle Trail north to junction with Northwest Basin Trail; Northwest Basin Trail to Hamlin Ridge Trail to Hamlin Peak. Descend Hamlin Ridge Trail to Chimney Pond Trail and Roaring Brook Campground.
- Markers: Blue blazes.
- Maintainer: BSP.
- Distance to Hamlin Peak summit: 6.8 miles.
- Start/finish Roaring Brook Campground: 11.3 miles.

This loop itinerary is a frequent choice of hikers seeking to summit both Katahdin and Hamlin Peak in the same day. It places the Knife Edge crossing early in the hike, after approaching the tree line and Pamola Peak via the Helon Taylor Trail.

After attaining the Katahdin summit, the route descends 1.1 miles to the low point in the saddle, where the Saddle Trail turns right (east) to descend to Chimney Pond. The loop continues with the ascent of Hamlin Peak via a 0.9-mile stretch of the Northwest Basin Trail and 0.2 mile on Hamlin Peak Cutoff.

The descent is via Hamlin Ridge Trail, North Basin Trail, North Basin Cutoff, and Chimney Pond Trail to Roaring Brook.

If unfavorable weather discourages a Hamlin descent, the Saddle Trail to Chimney Pond remains an option, and the party will have completed a hike to the Katahdin summit.

It is essential to consult a weather forecast and trail-status notice for the summit area before beginning a hike on Katahdin. Weather at high elevation may be utterly different from that at the base of the mountains. Such information is available at https://baxterstatepark.org or by calling 207-723-5140. Weather forecasts are posted at ranger stations in the park.

Cathedral Trail: Chimney Pond Campground to Katahdin Summit

This striking trail ascends three prominent outcrops rising above Chimney Pond, known as the Cathedrals. It is the most direct route to the summit, following a near fall line between Chimney Pond and the peak. I have hiked it a number of times and treasure the dramatic cliff-side views and the oh-so-close look at intricate features of the Great Basin.

Some hikers choose the Cathedral Trail because it is 0.2 mile shorter than the Saddle Trail. However, most hikers find that greater time is required to ascend Katahdin by the Cathedrals because of the persistent steepness. Expect hiking times in excess of one hour per mile on the Cathedral Trail.

Descending this trail is emphatically discouraged because lengthy steep pitches may be particularly difficult on descent.

Dudley Trail: Chimney Pond Campground to Pamola Peak and Knife Edge Trail to Katahdin Summit

The Dudley Trail, named for the late Baxter State Park supervisor, cutter of trails, and Maine Guide Roy Dudley, connects Chimney Pond Campground with Pamola Peak and the Knife Edge. For park visitors staying at Chimney Pond, the Dudley Trail makes possible a loop hike from the pond to the tableland and Katahdin summit, and then back to Chimney Pond.

The vantage point of the Dudley Trail, high to the east of the summit, provides unique views into the Great Basin and up to the Knife Edge and Katahdin summit. Ascent is quite steep, gaining 2,000 feet over a 2.4-mile distance from Chimney Pond, with hiking times comparable to those of the Cathedral Trail (i.e., 1 mile per hour or more).

Dudley Trail, closed in 2018 because of rock movement on the route, reopened in September 2020 following challenging rerouting and reconstruction performed by Baxter Park trail crews. Because of steepness, hiking times on Dudley Trail may be same whether descending or ascending. Contact Baxter State Park for details, including length, nature of terrain, and anticipated hiking times for the new route: https://baxterstatepark.org.

ALONE AT THE TOP

I have been summiting Katahdin for decades, have reached the summit in every season of the year, and have hiked every trail on the mountain. In the process, I have known Katahdin in many of its moods—clear see-forever days, the roaring cloud factory Thoreau described, pelting rain, a full-bore snowstorm, staggering sideways winds. On every occasion when I reached the top, I either was in a hiking group or encountered other hikers gathered there—until one particular summer day.

On a June morning in 2017, on an annual ascent of Katahdin, I reach the summit sign and cairn by way of the Saddle Trail—and discover that I am alone! There is not a single person in sight. Save for the whisper of a light wind, there is no sound—just utter quiet. Sunlight beams through breaks in a partly cloudy sky. I am alone on the summit of Katahdin.

For a time, I look out, scan the horizon, look near to inspect the jumble of rock by my feet and then look out long, far, once more. Time, then, to sit on a rock, midway between sign and summit cairn—just sit, sit and look.

My appetite stirs. I pull a bagel sandwich and an apple from my pack. That act draws company—of a sort. A coal-black raven flies in, settling on a rock just beyond arm's reach, and eyes me—or, more probably, my food. With a polite gesture, I speak evenly to the raven with words of welcome, adding that I will not be handing out lunch but that there is ample raven food to be had on the nearby tableland.

The raven looks at me, then looks out, and remains perched on that nearby rock. I, too, sit and look out. So it is that just the two of us, the raven and I, perch looking out to see what there is to see, with the summit of Katahdin all to ourselves. There we remain for a good half hour, until hikers appear from the direction of South Peak. I gather my gear together, rise, and step in the direction of the still-unpeopled Saddle Trail for my descent. The raven departs. I speak words of farewell as it wings its way in the direction of the Knife Edge. Goodbye for now, my summit companion. Goodbye, until we meet again, *Ktaadin*.

Western Approaches

The Hunt Trail and the Abol Trail—which joins the Hunt Trail by the top of the Abol Slide at Thoreau Spring—are the two approaches from the west. The AT follows the Hunt Trail to the summit of Katahdin. On any given day, expect to see long-distance AT hikers pass through Katahdin Stream trailhead, heading north or south, as part of their 2,192-mile journey.

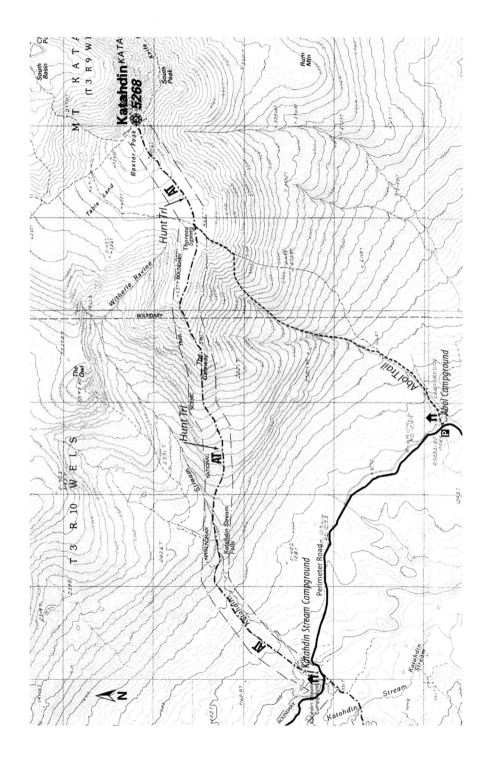

Of the two trailheads, Katahdin Stream is the busier, as it is used by day hikers and AT hikers. The campground at Katahdin Stream serves as a base camp for hikers staying in the park for one or more nights, perhaps undertaking multiple-peak hikes in this western region of the park. The parking area is substantially larger than that at Abol trailhead, which is 2.0 miles east of Katahdin Stream—but it does fill at times. Day hikers driving into the park are urged to obtain a parking reservation prior to arrival.

Trails
Hunt Trail/Appalachian Trail North

The Hunt Trail provides extraordinary views of a pond and peak array immediately west of Katahdin and well beyond over the Hundred-Mile Wilderness, the Debsco-neag Lakes, Jo-Mary Lake, and so many other waters, to White Cap Mountain and the Gulf Hagas Range 70 miles distant. From the top of the Southwest Spur—also known as Hunt Spur—on the tableland, views extend northward to the Brothers and Cross Ranges, down into the great Klondike Bog and Pond, and up to Katahdin itself.

Along the way the route passes 80-foot-high Katahdin Stream Falls and negotiates an extraordinary steep boulder-field section of trail requiring many a scramble and frequent four-point work. Iron rungs and footholds have been affixed to the rock to aid the passage. Final ascent to the spur passes through the Gateway, two massive boulders at the edge of the tableland. Hikers here enter an upward-sloping, 1.5-mile otherworldly alpine zone—felsenmeer, sedge shaking in persistent wind. The Katahdin summit rises at the height of that slope, discernable by the summit cairn and square summit sign.

Abol Trail joins Hunt/AT North at Thoreau Spring for the final 1.0 mile to the peak. In the final approach, South Peak and the rock rubble of the trailless south wall of Katahdin enter into view. The trail ends abruptly, which seems appropriate, at the very edge of the Great Basin, where, a few steps from the top, the east edge of Katahdin falls away in a precipitous drop of nearly 2,000 feet to Chimney Pond. This is the highest point in Maine.

- Trailhead: Katahdin Stream Campground and ranger station, 8.3 miles west of Togue Pond Gate, on the Perimeter Road (also known as Nesowadnehunk Tote Road). Day-use parking is at the end of the camp road, on the left. Please do not park by campsites unless holding a reservation for that site. There is a hiker register on the porch of the ranger station, east of the parking and camping areas, across a footbridge over Katahdin Stream. Register when you begin the hike and upon return.
- The trailhead (prominent sign) is at the north side of the parking area.
- Markers: White blazes.
- Maintainer: BSP, MATC.

- Distance to summit: 5.5 miles (11.0 miles RT).
- Points of interest:
    Katahdin Stream trailhead.
    Trail to the Owl, a 3,670-foot peak overlooking the Klondike.
    Katahdin Stream footbridge below Katahdin Stream Falls.
    2.0 O-Joy Brook.
    3.0 Hunt Spur; beginning of boulder section.
    3.6 The Gateway.
    3.7 Tableland.
    4.5 Junction with Abol Trail at Thoreau Spring.
    5.5 Katahdin summit: 5,268 feet.

My very first ascent of Katahdin was via the Hunt Trail. I prize this route for the ruggedness of the climb and that remarkable moment when I step out onto the tableland, the scrambling done for a time and the high, wild alpine zone a great sweep ahead of me, rising to the summit. The view into the Klondike captivates me as well, this vast trailless wetland, headwater to Wassataquoik Stream, fed by rain and snowmelt off Katahdin and the Brothers Range. The waters gather and pause in this great mountain bog before running down to meet the East Branch of the Penobscot River, the Penobscot itself, and then the distant sea.

I start early, by headlamp, moments ahead of 6:00 a.m. and am not first on the trail. Others have signed in and departed, headlamps bobbing ahead, up the trail. Katahdin Stream rushes by in the darkness, off to my right. Katahdin Stream Falls announce themselves well in advance of my arrival at the footbridge. I pause here on the return hike. The falls are too good to miss. In late afternoon the sun hits the falling waters straight on. Quite the sight.

The way ascends steadily. Steadily turns to steeply. I stop every sixty minutes to drink water and to eat some apple slices, part of a bagel, or half a homemade power bar.

Boulder time. One foothold at a time—no rush. Set myself, push off, up, up, up. The rungs and footholds are strategically placed. There is a short line of hikers waiting a turn. Above this point there is more rock work to be done, but the steepness eases, if only a bit. I take time for the views, which run for at least 100 miles on a clear day.

The Gateway stands ahead, where the pathway passes between two great granite slabs to reach the tableland. The view opens up across the vast tableland, a wild expanse of fractured rock interspersed with alpine flowers—sandwort, dependable diapensia, sedge. The summit of Katahdin looms to the east edge of the tableland, visible below blue sky, suddenly hidden as clouds drop swirl, and then visible again as the wind drives the clouds away.

I resume the hike, 1.8 miles remaining to reach the summit. Thoreau Spring is a marker, a reminder that I am making progress. Sometimes there is enough water here to draw some, but I do not depend on this spring as a water source; I carry an ample supply. At the spring the Abol Trail enters from the right (south). There are days when I have ascended Abol and descended Hunt, or vice versa, for the variety of footpath and different angles of view. Each route has its appeal, and typically I ascend one and descend the other.

On to the summit, the ascent now a walk up a long, gently rising rock staircase. I am there! The sign, weathered; the high cairn, perched at the lip of the Great Basin; the Knife Edge—undulating rock and spires—arcing off toward Pamola Peak. People whose accents and language are signs that hikers have come here from across the nation and around the world. There are those who laugh, those who sing, those who step away from the summit gathering to sit quietly. *Ktaadn.*

Abol Trail: Abol Campground to Thoreau Spring; Katahdin via Hunt Trail

Abol Trail has been rerouted following movement on the Abol Slide in 2013. The original approach to the slide at the beginning of the route and the uppermost section of the slide remain part of the route.

The new middle section of Abol Trail represents one of the finer works of trail construction I have seen anywhere and represents a new standard for hiking trails in the northeastern United States. A traverse, rock staircases, a major switchback, rock water bars, a well-chosen flat-rock viewing point—careful thought and execution are evident here.

Lest anyone think this is now just a walk in the park, the elevation gain is similar to that on the Hunt Trail: 3,900 feet from trailhead to summit. The trail returns to the Abol Slide for a 0.1-mile scramble up and over sloping edge, boulders, and scree before it reaches the tableland, Thoreau Spring, and the Hunt Trail. The summit lies 1.0 mile ahead on the Hunt Trail—marked on clear days by the summit sign and cairn. On other days, the clouds race over the summit, propelled by winds sweeping in from the north or west over the tableland or up through the great east-lying cirques or between the steep, trailless ridges that fall off to the south.

Even with the reroute, Abol Trail remains the shortest-distance road-to-summit trail on the Katahdin massif. For hikers seeking to spend a night in the park in order to get an early start, if the campgrounds at Abol and Katahdin Stream are full, the self-service cabins at Daicey Pond and Kidney Pond and the lean-tos and tent sites at Nesowadnehunk Campground are good options.

- Trailhead: Abol Campground and ranger station, 6.3 miles on Perimeter Road west of Togue Pond Gate. Limited-space day-use parking on left (south) side of the road, across from the ranger station. Hiker register on porch.
- Markers: Blue blazes.

- Maintainer: BSP.
- Distance to summit: 4.4 miles (8.8 miles RT).
- Points of interest:
  Abol ranger station.
  Trailhead (sign) at north end of campground.
  1.0 Reroute angles left (west).
  2.4 Viewing point.
  2.6 Tree line.
  3.4 Thoreau Spring; junction with Hunt Trail.
  4.4 Katahdin summit: 5,268 feet.

In the reroute, the trail ascends by a long westward traverse, at a grade that moves water off the trail but invites a steady walking pace. Rock staircases ascend unavoidable steep sections. Obvious thought has been given to step installation and the rise of each step. The footpath has been worked out of the hillside to minimize root intrusion and limit erosion—less work for trail maintainers, fewer slips (perhaps) for hikers.

A major switchback—rare on New England trails—brings me to a viewing point at 2.4 miles, where flat-topped boulders at the edge of a fir-bordered clearing provide a front-row seat to the vast lake country, the Hundred-Mile Wilderness, and the peaks this side of Moosehead Lake—Big and Little Spencer to the southwest.

Back on trail, I am at tree line in 0.2 mile, return to the ascent, and reach the upper section of Abol Slide. Back to work: Careful foot placement, haul up, more of the same—I rise into a bank of swirling clouds and top out a few yards from Thoreau Spring. In his account of his ascent to this point, Thoreau wrote of Katahdin as a cloud factory. The factory is churning out the clouds on my day, as it did on his.

I have the clothing and gear for this. Stepping to the lee of a boulder, I put on a down sweater and add a breathable wind and rain shell. On goes the wool cap, a neck warmer, and gloves, and I am on my way, wind whipping my face, buffeting the sleeves of my jacket. I enjoy this, the mountain on its terms. Clouds part, close in again, great sheets of mist roll across the tableland. A shaft of sunlight. Back and forth it goes.

The summit! I have come to this *Ktaadn* so many times. I still get a charge out of it, this high, rocky place, clouds and sun and shafts of light all about.

Abol Trail on Ascent, Hunt Trail on Descent, or Vice Versa

On some of my Katahdin ascents from the west, I have gone up one trail and down the other. I appreciate the terrain and views unique to each. Weather influences my decision, of course.

Abol Trail ascent: I favor this when weather is uncertain or might deteriorate in the course of the day. It is also my choice when hiking with a group of people whose hiking experience varies. Or I may simply take this trail for its own particular beauty and long views. Once at the tableland or at the summit, I consider the hours of remaining daylight, the weather, and my energy level. If those seem favorable, I will head down the Hunt Trail. The views into the Klondike and beyond to the Brothers Range are exceptional. I do not want to miss them, and they are well worth the extra mile difference between the two trails.

The Hunt Trail descent takes time and requires that all-important foot placement but is less tiring for me than a Hunt Trail ascent.

Hunt Trail ascent: The route is more demanding physically than the Abol Trail. By hiking it when fresh and planning to descend via Abol Trail, I expect to have the more difficult trail work behind me by midday. I have special memories of family hikes and of my AT hike on the Hunt Trail—and how often do I get to haul myself using rungs and iron footholds?

If wet weather threatens, I would not ascend (or descend) this way. Although I have hiked many a rainy mile in the Maine mountains and been on Katahdin when rain and snow have blown in, I now avoid a Katahdin ascent in poor weather. Footing becomes very difficult in wet conditions. I will return on a better day.

Northern Approaches

Two routes approach Katahdin from the north, climbing out of the interior of the park from Russell Pond Campground to reach Katahdin over long, exposed stretches of tableland: Northwest Basin Trail, which passes remote Davis Pond and its lean-to camp, and the North Peaks Trail, which has no campsite along the route.

Park procedures require that hiking parties camp overnight at an established BSP site before hiking these trails, making northern approach hikes backpacking trips. The usual campsite for this arrangement is Russell Pond Campground, in the interior of the park, which has lean-tos, tent sites, and a bunkhouse.

The Northwest Basin Trail developed in a two-step process when two couples, Roy and Abby Dudley and Frank and Grace Butcher, led a trail-cutting effort and constructed the first rough shelter by Davis Pond in the early 1930s. Roy gained legendary status as the game warden stationed at Chimney Pond. As recounted by John Neff in the book *Katahdin: An Historic Journey* (see "Good Reads," appendix F), the two couples had bushwhacked to Davis Pond in a previous year, were struck by its remote beauty, and decided to lead a trail construction effort. As the story goes, some years later a separate party cut a trail up from the Russell Pond area to Davis Pond to complete a through-trail.

The North Peaks Trail was once considered a potential primary route to bring visitors to Katahdin, with a hotel proposed near the North Tableland and a horse trail constructed to lead from the Russell Pond area to Katahdin. Once called the Tracy Path, the route fell out of favor before it became a reality when new routes opened on the south and west side of Katahdin, which were closer to railroad and wagon access near Millinocket.

Remoteness

In a park already remote, these are the most remotely located trails to cross extended stretches of boulder field and alpine terrain. Both are lightly traveled. The footpaths are rough, steep, and often slippery because snow comes early and lingers long in the north-lying draws and on north-facing slopes. Long after the last snows let up, the trails remain wet, even in steep sections. A ford of Wassataquoik Stream, South Branch, must be made on either trail, a difficult (if not impossible) maneuver during spring runoff and after heavy rain.

Both of these trails—Northwest Basin Trail and North Peaks Trail—are lightly traveled. The Davis Pond lean-to is limited to one party per night and a one-night stay. The North Peaks Trail has no campsite along its route, and it is common for days to pass with no hikers using this trail. Above the tree line some route-finding may be required. Although the trails are blue-blazed and marked by cairns above tree line, the pathway underfoot—particularly on the North Peaks Trail—is only lightly worn in sections. In conditions of low visibility, cairns may be difficult to distinguish.

Self-rescue skills, gear, and supplies are essential for either of these routes. Expect no cell phone service.

For those who do come here, properly experienced and equipped, either or both of these trails offer the hike of a lifetime. These two routes, for all their difficulty, are my two favorite trails on Katahdin because of the wildness of the setting and the stark beauty of the Northwest Basin, Northwest Plateau, North Tableland, and North Peaks.

Backpacking from the North
Northwest Basin Trail

As indicated above, the Davis Pond lean-to is limited to one party per night, for a maximum one-night stay. BSP requires that Davis Pond campers (Northwest Basin Trail) spend the previous night at another campsite, which is almost always Russell Pond. The night after Davis Pond might best be spent at Chimney Pond Campground to avoid a very long hike out to Roaring Brook Campground.

Russell Pond Overnight Stay

To reach Russell Pond, hikers usually depart from Roaring Brook Campground and ranger station and hike the 6.8-mile Russell Pond Trail or the 7.2-mile Wassataquoik Stream Trail variation. The latter diverges from the Russell Pond Trail after 3.1 miles, joining it again after meeting and crossing the main branch of the stream, where two lean-tos are located.

Sign the hiker register at Russell Pond, located at a kiosk at the edge of the campground in a small clearing. Do this when arriving at Russell Pond and when departing for the hike the next day. Inform the ranger of your plans to hike the Northwest Basin Trail or the North Peaks Trail.

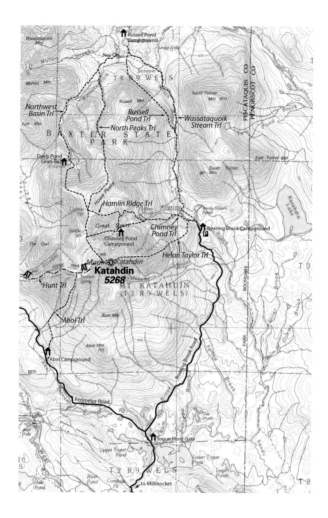

Trails

Northwest Basin Trail: Russell Pond Trail to Northwest Basin Trail to Davis Pond; from Davis Pond via Northwest Basin Trail to Saddle Trail to Katahdin; Descent to Chimney Pond via Saddle Trail

- Trailhead: Russell Pond Campground.
- Markers: Blue blazes, cairns.
- Maintainer: BSP.
- Distance to Katahdin summit: 9.6 miles; to Chimney Pond after Katahdin summit: 11.6 miles.
- Points of interest:
    Russell Pond Campground, Russell Pond Trail; hiker register at campground kiosk.

0.1 Junction, Northwest Basin Trail.

1.2 North Peaks Trail junction. Continue on Northwest Basin Trail.

2.6 Annis Brook.

3.7 Ford Wassataquoik Stream.

4.9 Lake Cowles.

5.2 Davis Pond lean-to.

7.6 Hamlin Peak Cutoff; Caribou Spring spur trail.

8.5 Saddle Trail junction.

9.6 Katahdin summit: 5,268 feet.

To hike the Northwest Basin Trail is to enter a wilderness setting that I compare with locations in Alaska, the Sierras, and the Rockies—particularly the Western Slope of the Rockies, where at one point in my life I made repeated backpack trips to remote high-country lakes reached over unmarked trails. Davis Pond and nearby Lake Cowles (a pond in size) stand at the bottom of the Northwest Basin, another of the many great glacial cirques cut into the tableland.

The extensive treeless terrain, sharp walls of the cirque, and utter remoteness are rare in eastern North America. I am quite taken by this interior terrain in the park. Of all places I have hiked anywhere in the world, Northwest Basin is one of my favorites. Ascending to and beyond this spot is work—rewarding work.

My hike begins uneventfully, with passage along the Wassataquoik. I plan my hikes from the north to Katahdin for mid- to late summer, when stream flows are down. I ford Wassataquoik Stream with care and begin the trek out of that valley along a long draw and sometimes right up a streambed. There is water flow here, not deep but sufficient to make for slippery conditions. At times I step away from the stream to bushwhack through thick growth, after doing a few dance steps on slick rock. I climb out of this section, ascend steadily, and reach Lake Cowles. The outlet at the north end of the lake has been partially obstructed by the work of beavers. I cross the outlet on the lower beaver dam and step to the *roches moutonnées*—glacier-sculpted, sheepback ledge outcrops above the east shore. With a gentle slope at one end and a sharper slope at the other, they resemble the backs of sheep lying in pasture. As a sheep farmer, of Cotswold and Rambouillet, I see the likeness!

Once a lean-to stood on this rise by the *roches*, and I overnighted in it. The location is striking, with a view of the Northwest Basin straight ahead to the south, the great cliff wall along the North Tableland to the east, and Lake Cowles and a view toward the Brothers Range to the west. Alas, that was a bit too much exposure for the three-sided lean-to when winter storm winds converged on this spot. A park ranger told me that trail crews would arrive in spring to find the lean-to blown sideways; one year they discovered it tipped on its back by those winds.

The lean-to now is located up the trail in a sheltered hollow. I explore that hollow, follow the sound of falling water to discover a high, horsetail waterfall dropping into the Northwest Basin, and fall asleep to water music. A wild and remote natural amphitheater!

My hike toward Katahdin continues in the morning, with a steep climb up the east side of the basin, where I ascend through runoff on slippery ledge. At the most challenging stretches of the route, I take to the adjacent woods, where the terrain is also steep but offers some ground to plant my feet, as I work my way upward.

Next is a boulder field, as the route moves out of the basin and onto the tableland. I exchange slippery conditions underfoot for a stop-and-go pace as I work my way around and over the rock. I am loving the wild nature of all this. It is a good thing that I do, as once on the tableland I am buffeted by strong tableland winds, low cloud ceiling, and off-and-on rain. Ah, the many moods of Katahdinauguoh!

Rain jacket, rain pants, wool cap, neck warmer, gloves: Donning these, I continue toward Hamlin Peak, with the slopes of the Howe Peaks—in the shape of outlandishly sized *roches moutonnées*—above me, to the east. All around me are rock, sedge, tiny alpine flowers—diapensia and sandwort among them. Before me, a line of cairns trails off into the distance.

I follow that line over the shoulder of Hamlin, down into the saddle, and up to Katahdin.

North Peaks Trail: Russell Pond Trail to Northwest Basin Trail to North Peaks Trail; over the North/Howe Peaks to Saddle Trail and Katahdin. Descend to Chimney Pond via Saddle Trail

- Trailhead: Russell Pond Campground.
- Markers: Blue blazes, cairns.
- Maintainer: BSP.
- Distance to Katahdin summit: 8.9 miles; to Chimney Pond after Katahdin summit: 11.1 miles.
- Points of interest:
    Russell Pond Campground; Russell Pond Trail; hiker register at campground kiosk.
    0.1 Junction with Northwest Basin Trail.
    1.2 North Peaks Trail junction. Turn left (south).
    1.5 Ford Wassataquoik Stream.
    4.9 First high point north of Howe Peaks.
    5.7 North-lying Howe Peak.
    6.2 South-lying Howe Peak.
    6.7 Hamlin Peak Cutoff.
    6.9 Northwest Basin Trail junction.

7.8 Saddle Trail junction.

8.9 Katahdin summit: 5,268 feet.

11.1 Chimney Pond, after descent by Saddle Trail.

The North Peaks Trail departs from the Northwest Basin Trail a forty-five-minute walk from Russell Pond. I pick my way across the Turner Deadwater outlet over dry-ki and beaver flotsam but maintain my balance. Trekking poles help. The ford of Wassataquoik Stream is more formidable. I hike early in July, and the stream still runs deep.

To prepare for the crossing, I change out of my hiking shoes and into closed-toe river sandals. I loosen my backpack waist, chest, and shoulder straps—in order to slip quickly from the pack if I fall in. I look the stream over and locate a route where the water seems shallowest. With a trekking pole in each hand, I face upstream and move laterally, one foot, then the other. Move one trekking pole, then the other. At all times I have at least three points of contact. The water in the deepest holes is thigh high.

Across, I change footgear and climb along the course of Tracy Brook—named for members of the Tracy family who ran logging operations in the Russell Pond area, built a sporting camp to attract guests, and saw great tourist potential if an approach trail to Katahdin could be developed from the north. Their dreams were not realized, but their efforts did result in establishment of what is now the North Peaks Trail.

After crossing Tracy Brook, the trail enters the gap between two low peaks at the north end of the North Tableland. Russell Mountain stands to the east. Tip-Top, a name that may signify its location at the edge of the Wassataquoik Valley below and the tableland above, is the low peak to the west. When I emerge from the last of the forest growth, I concentrate on locating the cairns ahead. The dark rock of the cairns is similar to that of the surrounding rock. The pathway is little worn, as this trail receives little hiker traffic. Therein lies its attraction—to hike in one of the remotest and least visited corners of the park.

The Howe Peaks appear ahead. I have ascended to an elevation well over 4,000 feet, but these two peaks rise only marginally above the surrounding ridge. There is not sufficient elevation difference from summits to ridge to qualify as 4,000-Footers. Instead, they are considered part of the slope that leads to Hamlin Peak.

I take a break on South Howe Peak, find a windbreak rock, sit in the midst of the treeless expanse, look out, look, and look. Next, I descend the modest slope of the Howe Peaks toward Caribou Spring to refresh my water supply, bypassing Hamlin. I have given Hamlin its due on many a previous Baxter State Park trip and will do so again—just not today. For now, it is on to Katahdin and down the Saddle Trail to overnight camp at Chimney Pond.

End of the Trail: Additional and Helpful Information

Out of the Ordinary

Pursue the Maine 4,000-Footers in an out-of-the-ordinary way! Reach the summits of 4,000-foot peaks not on the Four-Thousand-Footer Club (FTFC) list. Backpack the 4,000-foot peaks on overnight trips. Start the planning process to summit the peaks in winter. Combine fishing for brook trout with your mountain trek.

Overlooked: 4,000-Footers Off the List

To qualify for the New England 4,000-Footer list, if there are two or more peaks above 4,000 feet on the same ridge, the lower-elevation peak must rise at least 200 feet above the separating col. If this were not the case, each point of high ground along a ridge could qualify, adding dozens more peaks to the list—which are not truly separate mountains. On Saddleback, for example, three such promontories stand on the summit ridge. The highest one bears the summit sign. This is common sense.

A handful of named Maine peaks, reached by strenuous ascent and exceeding 4,000 feet in elevation, do not qualify. All are in Baxter State Park (BSP), and all are located on either the Knife Edge or the North Tableland.

Knife Edge Peaks: Pamola, Chimney, and South Peaks

Pamola Peak, 4,912 feet, stands at the east end of the Knife Edge. Beside it, across the sharp gap of Chimney Col, is 4,900-foot Chimney Peak. The third summit, South Peak, comes oh-so-close to Katahdin's 5,268-foot elevation, falling just short at 5,240 feet. Seen from some angles, South Peak is sometimes mistaken as the higher point.

Hikers completing the Knife Edge Trail proceed over all three summits, gaining elevation over the 1.1-mile distance from Pamola to Katahdin and losing elevation when going from Katahdin to Pamola. The serrated conformation of the Knife Edge—sometimes referred to as Knife Teeth—is such that there are multiple elevation gains and losses en route. However, none of these dramatic serrations meet the standard of a 200-foot elevation gain above an intervening col.

The Howe Peaks

Another set of Baxter State Park 4,000-foot-plus peaks that do not qualify as New England 4,000-Footers are the Howe Peaks, also known as the North Peaks, on the North Tableland. Three points of high ground stand in a north-to-south line north of Hamlin Peak at elevations of 4,182 feet, 4,612 feet, and 4,734 feet. The name Howe Peaks is usually used to refer to the highest two summits closest to Hamlin Peak. All occupy the alpine zone, a vast area of tableland rock rubble and sedge, and they all have open summits. However, they have little prominence above the tableland and are regarded by Four-Thousand-Footer Club standards as approach points to Hamlin Peak from the north and not as separately defined peaks.

The Howe Peaks are named for Burton Howe, a friend of Percival Baxter who was instrumental in introducing Baxter to the extraordinary lands that now compose

Baxter State Park. In the late 1800s and early 1900s, the trail that passes over these peaks was a significant approach route to Katahdin, but it was discontinued for a variety of reasons—the essence of which is that other, more accessible trails became available on the east and west slopes of Katahdin, with their own compelling landscapes.

The landscape is remarkable, compelling—and utterly wild: rock, sedge, scattered patches of krummholz, distant views, buffeting winds. I prize the Howe Peaks for their remoteness and rough-edged beauty.

Because a hike to these distant summits adds mileage to an already long and strenuous hike for those summiting Katahdin, Hamlin, or both, few hikers include the North Peaks on an itinerary. See the section in this book on "Katahdin—Northern Approaches" for North Peaks Trail information.

Caution: These peaks are completely exposed, and the trails reaching them are rough and rocky. They can be dangerous in rain, snow, ice, fog, and high wind. Weather conditions may obscure trail blazes and cairns. Sound navigation skills are essential.

Consult with Baxter State Park authorities to plan a hike that includes the Howe Peaks.

Backpacking Maine's 4,000-Footers

Maine's 4,000-foot peaks and the ranges where they rise offer dozens of backpacking options. What follows is a sample of common point-to-point, out-and-back, and loop trips. Point-to-point hikes may be traveled in either direction. Similarly, loop hikes may be taken clockwise or counterclockwise. Specific local features may make one direction more favorable than another.

For trip planning, see trail descriptions in this book for individual peaks. Appendix F, "Good Reads," lists additional long-distance hiking resources, such as the *Appalachian Trail Thru-Hikers Companion* (2021).

Mahoosuc Range: Shelburne, New Hampshire, to Grafton Notch, Maine

4,000-foot peak: Old Speck	**Distance:** 31.0 miles
Trail: Appalachian Trail (AT)/Mahoosuc Range	**Campsites/lean-to (south to north):** Trident Col (tents only), Gentian Pond,
Point-to-point hike	Carlo Col, Full Goose, Speck Pond

The Mahoosuc Range traverse is one of the outstanding rugged ridge hikes in eastern North America. While Old Speck is the sole 4,000-Footer, intervening peaks, including Mt. Carlo, Goose Eye, Fulling Mill, and Mahoosuc Arm, are all above 3,500 feet in elevation, with remarkable views over exceptionally wild terrain.

The rocky high ground of Mt. Carlo; remote waters of Dream Lake, Gentian Pond, and Speck Pond; high mountain bogs north of Goose Eye; great stretches of krummholz; and the otherworldly jumble of Mahoosuc Notch are among the rewards awaiting hikers. Expect to require more hiking time than usual over this terrain.

Those seeking a shorter backpacking hike may approach the Mahoosuc Range from a number of trails that lead from the Success Pond Road, north of the range. This road leads northeast from Berlin, New Hampshire.

Grafton Notch, West Section

4,000-foot peak: Old Speck **Trail:** Grafton Loop Trail **Point-to-point hike** **Distance:** West Section: 17.1 miles **Campsites:** Bald Mountain, Sargent Brook, Slide Mountain, Bull Run; tents only; no fires; privy	**Fee:** Grafton Notch State Park seasonal self-pay station at AT/Old Speck parking area, Highway 26 parking area (*Note:* No camping in Grafton Notch State Park)

The West Section runs from a trailhead at lower Grafton Notch, 4.9 miles north of US Route 2, on Highway 26 in Newry, Maine, to the AT/Old Speck trailhead in Grafton Notch State Park, which is 12.0 miles north of US Route 2. This West Section passes over Old Speck summit; the East Section does not. A major feature of the West Section is Sunday River Whitecap, elevation 3,335 feet, where there are striking views of the Mahoosuc, Carter-Moriah, and Presidential Ranges, as well as the sharp cut of Grafton Notch and the east-lying Baldpate Range.

The distance from the trailhead to Old Speck summit via the west side of the loop is 13.3 miles. From the Old Speck summit to Grafton Notch AT trailhead is another 3.8 miles, for a total of 17.1 miles. The final 3.8 miles are a descent of the Old Speck route described in the "Mahoosuc Range" chapter.

The loop trail was constructed to provide options for hikers to visit the Old Speck and Baldpate region without relying solely on the Appalachian Trail. The West Section of Grafton Loop Trail, which reaches the Old Speck summit, opened in 2007 and followed construction of the earlier-built East Section, which opened in 2003. The loop trail offers tent sites, which makes backpacking in the region possible, as there is no camping permitted in Grafton Notch State Park.

The East Section from the Newry trailhead to the AT/Old Speck trailhead parking lot in Grafton Notch State Park covers 21.1 miles and does not cross the summit of Old Speck, which is on the *west* side of the Notch. To reach Old Speck summit, while completing an east-to-west loop, from the AT parking area, continue on the AT South on the day-hike route described in the "Old Speck" section of this book. Reach the summit in 3.8 miles. Continue south on the west loop for an additional 13.3 miles to return to the Newry trailhead, using one of the designated campsites along the way.

Saddleback Range: Maine Highway 4 (South of Rangeley) to Redington Stream Tent Site

4,000-foot peaks: Saddleback and The Horn
Trails: AT North (AT South on return)
Out-and-back hike

Distance: 8.0 miles (16.0 miles RT)
Campsites/lean-to: Piazza Rock, Redington Stream (tents only)

Hike the Saddleback Range without pressure of time to fit the miles within a day hike. From the AT Redington Stream tent site, walk 0.3 mile back up to the AT to watch the sunset from the Saddleback ridge. Awake to sunrise on the high ground. Start with an overnight at the Piazza Rock campsite to awake already in the mountains, or camp at both sites for maximum time to enjoy the Saddleback Range.

Saddleback to Sugarloaf: Maine Highway 4 to Caribou Pond Road

4,000-foot peaks: Saddleback, The Horn, Mt. Abraham, Spaulding, Sugarloaf
Trails: AT North; spur trails to Abraham, Spaulding, and Sugarloaf
Point-to-point hike

Distance: 24.0 miles
Campsites/lean-to: Piazza Rock, Redington Stream (tents only), Poplar Ridge, Spaulding Mountain

Summit five 4,000-footers in a hike with 2–3 overnights.

Mt. Abraham: Caribou Pond Road off Maine Highway 27

4,000-foot peaks: Mt. Abraham, Spaulding, Sugarloaf (via spur trail)
Trails: Fire Warden Trail, Mt. Abraham Trail, AT North
Point-to-point hike

Distance: 11.9 miles
Campsites/lean-to: Fire Warden Trail campsite (tents only); Spaulding Mountain lean-to

Summit the interior peaks of Abraham and Spaulding and add Sugarloaf from its wilder south side. Overnight at the Fire Warden Trail tent site and/or Spaulding Mountain campsite to spread the distance over multiple days and allow extra time on the summits or in leisurely camps. Arrange a vehicle shuttle.

Saddleback Range to Crocker Range: Maine Highway 4 to Maine Highway 27

4,000-foot peaks: Saddleback, The Horn, Mt. Abraham, Spaulding, Sugarloaf, South Crocker, Redington, North Crocker **Trails:** AT North; spur trails to Abraham, Spaulding, Sugarloaf, Redington herd paths	**Point-to-point hike** **Distance:** 36.0 miles **Campsites/lean-to:** Piazza Rock, Redington Stream (tents only), Poplar Ridge, Spaulding Mountain, Crocker Cirque (tents only)

Complete a hike of all eight 4,000-foot peaks between Highway 4, south of Rangeley, and the Highway 27 AT crossing in Wyman Township. There are AT parking areas and signed trailheads at either end of this itinerary.

AT North is the principal route. Spur trails lead to all off-AT summits. Allow three to four nights. Arrange vehicle shuttle.

Mt. Abraham Out-and-Back

4,000-foot peaks: Abraham, Spaulding **Trails:** Fire Warden Trail; Mt. Abraham spur trail to AT **Out-and-back hike**	**Distance:** 15.6 miles RT **Campsites/lean-to:** Fire Warden Trail tent site and/or Spaulding Mountain campsite (lean-to and tent site)

Hikers may shorten the distance to be covered in a given day on the Fire Warden Trail by making camp at the Maine Appalachian Trail Club campsite 2.6 miles from the Rapid Stream trailhead. Site: privy; fire pit; water from stream; cleared but otherwise unimproved tent sites. Day hike the remaining 1.6 miles to Mt. Abraham summit on following day and hike back out. Day one: 2.6 miles; day two: 6.4 miles.

To include Spaulding Mountain, continue beyond Mt. Abraham on Mt. Abraham spur trail to the AT. Hike AT North to Spaulding Mountain campsite, taking the Spaulding Mountain spur trail to that summit. Return hike to Rapid Stream trailhead. Day one: 2.6 miles; day two: 13.0 miles.

Divide the distance more evenly by hiking on day one to Mt. Abraham and on to Spaulding Mountain campsite for an overnight. On day two, summit Spaulding Mountain and return to the Rapid Stream trailhead via Mt. Abraham. Day one: 7.4 miles; day two: 8.2 miles.

Crocker Range and Redington Mountain: Caribou Pond Road Yellow Gate and Return

4,000-foot peaks: South Crocker, North Crocker, Redington
Trails: Caribou Pond Road to AT; AT North; South Crocker–Redington Saddle herd path; AT South

Loop/lollipop hike (Start/end same trail section; midportion of hike is a loop.)
Distance: 10.8 miles RT
Campsite: Crocker Cirque (tents only, on platforms); central fire pit; privy

This quirky itinerary has become popular with 4,000-foot peak-baggers. Hike from Yellow Gate to AT North to Crocker Cirque Campsite. Ascend South Crocker on AT North. Continue to North Crocker. Return to South Crocker. Hike on South Crocker–Redington Saddle herd path to ascend Redington. Return by herd path to South Crocker summit. Descend AT South to Caribou Pond Road and Yellow Gate. Day one: 1.5 miles; day two: 9.3 miles. *Five* 4,000-footer summits!

Bigelow Range: From Maine Highway 27 and Return

4,000-foot peaks: West Peak, Avery Peak (also New England Hundred Highest peak of Bigelow South Horn)
Trails: AT, Fire Warden Trail
Loop/lollipop hike (Start/end on same section of trail; hike a loop in the middle.)

Distance: 16.4 miles RT
Campsites/lean-to: Cranberry Stream (tents only), Horns Pond (lean-to and tent site), Avery Col (tents only), Moose Falls (tents only), Stratton Brook Pond (tents only)

Bigelow Range: Horns Pond–Avery Col Loop

4,000-foot peaks: West Peak, Avery Peak (also New England Hundred Highest peak Bigelow South Horn)
Trails: Fire Warden Trail (lower), Horns Pond Trail, AT North, Fire Warden Trail on descent

Loop/lollipop hike (Start/end on same section of trail; hike a loop in the middle.)
Distance: 13.4 miles RT
Campsites/lean-to: Horns Pond lean-to, Avery Col (tent site only), Moose Falls (tents only), Stratton Brook Pond (tents only)

The two Bigelow itineraries offer overnight alternatives to a day hike.

Northeast on Bigelow Range: Maine Highway 27 to East Flagstaff Road

4,000-foot peaks: West Peak, Avery Peak (New England Hundred Highest South Horn)
Trails: AT North, Safford Brook Trail
Point-to-point hike
Distance: 12.3 miles

Campsites/lean-to: Cranberry Stream (tents only), Horns Pond, Avery Col (tents only), Moose Falls (tents only), Stratton Brook Pond (tents only), Safford Notch (tents only), Round Barn site on Flagstaff Lake (tents only)

From AT crossing and trailhead Highway 27, Wyman Township, hike AT North into Bigelow Preserve. Choose AT North of Stratton Brook Pond Road or Fire Warden Trail as approach route. If following Fire Warden Trail, an option is to start at Fire Warden trailhead/Stratton Brook kiosk and parking area on Stratton Brook Pond Road.

Hike to overnight campsite of choice, before or after peak ascent(s). Avoid late arrival at Avery Col tent site, as space may be filled. On day two, hike AT North and Safford Brook Trail to Round Barn parking area, East Flagstaff Road. Arrange a vehicle shuttle.

Baxter State Park: Hamlin/Katahdin Loop via Chimney Pond from Roaring Brook

4,000-foot peaks: Katahdin, Hamlin
Trails: Chimney Pond Campground (CPC) from Roaring Brook Campground (RBC) via Chimney Pond Trail. Ascend Katahdin via Hamlin Ridge, Northwest Basin, and Saddle Trails. Return to Chimney Pond via Saddle Trail for second overnight or hike out to Roaring Brook Campground.
Loop hike

Distance: RBC to CPC, 3.2 miles; CPC to Hamlin Peak, 1.9 miles; Hamlin Peak to Katahdin, 2.1 miles; Katahdin to CPC via Saddle Trail, 2.2 miles; CPC to RBC, 3.2 miles (12.6 miles RT)
Campsite: Chimney Pond lean-tos or bunkhouse space by the bed; no tents
Fees and procedures: See https:// baxterstatepark.org

A Chimney Pond overnight breaks up a long day hike.

Northwest Basin Trail to Hamlin Peak, Katahdin

4,000-foot peaks: Katahdin, Hamlin
Trails: From Roaring Brook Campground: Wassataquoik Stream or Russell Pond Trails; Northwest Basin Trail; descend Saddle Trail and Chimney Pond Trail to Roaring Brook Campground

Loop hike
Distance: 20.8 miles RT
Campsites: Roaring Brook, Russell Pond, Davis Pond, Chimney Pond, Roaring Brook
Fees and procedures: https://baxter statepark.org

This remotely located route ascends Katahdin from the north out of Russell Pond and the Wassataquoik Valley, crossing some of the most rugged terrain in the park.

Camping at Roaring Brook on the night before the hike and the night ending allows extra time to complete the loop. Davis Pond requires a prior night at an interior site—in this case, Russell Pond (option: a Wassataquoik Stream lean-to), reached on day one.

Hike to Davis Pond, day two, via Northwest Basin Trail, allowing ample time, as this trail includes fording Wassataquoik Stream, hiking up running stream beds, and scrambling on rock pitches. Day two: Climb steeply out of Northwest Basin, negotiate boulder field, and cross tableland to Katahdin, with spur hike to Hamlin Peak. Descend by Saddle Trail to overnight at Chimney Pond or hike out to Roaring Brook.

Self-rescue skill and gear are essential for this itinerary.

Shelburne, New Hampshire, to Baxter State Park, or Reverse

4,000-foot peaks: All Maine 4,000-Footers
Trails: AT North (spur trails to Mt. Abraham, Spaulding, Sugarloaf, Redington) to Katahdin; Baxter State Park trails to Hamlin and North Brother

Point-to-point hike
Distance: Approximately 320 miles
Fees and procedures: https://baxterstatepark.org

A world-class through-hike of 3–4 weeks duration, with the route almost entirely on the AT and AT spur trails. Northbound: Consult with Baxter State Park authorities beforehand about access to trailheads for North Brother and Hamlin Peak for hikers entering BSP via the AT.

Reverse of this itinerary is an option. Southbound hikers might consider within-BSP transport to various trailheads by personal vehicle driven by someone who would exit BSP in the vehicle after the summiting of North Brother, Hamlin, and Katahdin. Remaining hiking party would proceed on foot south to Shelburne.

Overnight Camping Tips

Drinking Water
Water along the AT, in Bigelow Preserve, and in Baxter State Park, at all campsites, is from natural sources (stream, pond, lake, spring) and must be treated to be made potable.

Toilets

All sites listed have a vault toilet or privy.

Fires

Open fires are prohibited at specified sites on the AT, in the Bigelow Preserve, and in Baxter State Park. See websites or phone authorities to confirm.

Lean-to Use

Along the Appalachian Trail, lean-tos have been constructed for long-distance hikers who do not carry tents and depend upon them for shelter. Overnight campers should carry a tent, tent hammock, or tarp shelter and not depend upon a lean-to. Please do not set up a tent inside a lean-to, as this restricts space available to others.

The fact that a lean-to is not occupied when evening comes is no guarantee that hikers will not appear later. *Lean-to courtesy is to make room for others and never to expect exclusive use of the space for one's own hiking party.*

The lean-to use exception is in Baxter State Park, where one reserves a lean-to with a camping fee. It is thereby for the exclusive use of the reserving party. Tents may be set up in such lean-tos, but it is a good idea to consult with the camp ranger before doing so.

Pets

Pets are not allowed in Baxter State Park (https://baxterstatepark.org).

Some water sources on or near trails in this book are small springs or streams with limited flow in dry periods. Please keep dogs away from such sources. Carry a container from which your dog may drink.

Food Protection

Secure food by using a quality bear-resistant container or by hanging food from a high bear line where available in Baxter State Park. Rigging one's own high line is an option. Research how to do this effectively prior to the trip. If at a vehicle-accessible campsite, place food overnight inside the vehicle (preferably in the trunk if there is one).

Do not keep food in a tent or in a sleeping bag. Never leave food out, such as on a lean-to platform or bench, or on whatever rock, stump, or flat section of ground serves as makeshift table.

While bears are certainly a consideration, the more common threats to food supplies are mice, squirrels, skunks, and raccoons. If your food is stolen or becomes contaminated, it matters not whether the culprit is large or small.

Leave No Trace

You know this. Not a scrap of anything left behind. People get this concept now, and the mountains have become noticeably freer of wrappers, plastic bottles, orange peels, and such. Keep up the good work!

Winter Access

Winter is a magnificent time to be in Maine's high country. I am on snow, using cross-country skis, snowshoes, or boots with crampons, nearly every week in winter. A given hike may require use of all three modes of travel: skis to reach a trailhead, snowshoes for lower ascent, boots with crampons for the icy high ground.

Specific skills are essential for winter travel in the mountains. Such skills are beyond the scope of this publication.

Do note that every party entering the Maine mountains in winter must have the skill set specific to winter and be prepared for winter bivouac and for self-rescue. Some of the most difficult winter weather to be experienced in eastern North America occurs in these mountains.

If you are new to winter ascents, take a course in winter travel on foot and in winter camping. Go on a series of lower-level hikes with an experienced person before attempting to summit a 4,000-Footer in winter.

Before embarking on a winter ascent, obtain trail condition updates and weather forecasts from reliable sources. Most weather information is for communities near the mountains—not for the high ground. Baxter State Park and the Saddleback and Sugarloaf ski areas typically post both base and summit weather forecasts. Expect colder and windier weather at high elevations.

Practical Considerations for Winter Ascents

New England Four-Thousand-Footer Club Winter Qualification

Hikers seeking to qualify for Winter New England Four-Thousand-Footer Club status must complete every ascent in the season of winter as determined by the moment of the winter solstice in December and the moment of the spring equinox in March.

Winter on the Ground and in the Air, Despite the Calendar

First snows and icing conditions typically arrive in the Maine mountains in September. While early snows rarely last—they usually melt in warm days to follow—accumulations may mount quickly in a few hours and create dangerous conditions. I have encountered sleet in mid-July in the Bigelow Range, iced-over trails near Old Speck and on Mt. Abraham in September, and knee-deep snow with whiteout conditions on the Saddleback Range in early October. Snow has fallen in every month of the year in Baxter State Park.

In spring, snowfall may occur as late as May and early June. I have witnessed tents collapsed under the weight of overnight snow on Memorial Day weekend in Baxter State Park—and been greeted by bright sun, warm temperatures, and blackflies on the following day. While peaks viewed from afar appear to be free of most or all snow cover in spring, deep snow often remains on shaded slopes, in cols, and in ravines. Spring snow is usually rotten, resulting in "post-holing"—when a hiker's foot sinks knee or even thigh deep in soft snow, making travel arduous.

In 2019, the Abol Trail in Baxter State Park was closed because of snowpack until the first week of June. The Saddle Trail opening was delayed to Fourth of July week because of snowpack.

Access and Parking

Some of the trails in this collection are readily accessed in winter—but others are not. The remoteness of trailheads and the peaks themselves, unplowed roads and parking areas, sections prone to icing and deep snow drifts, and the absence of footbridges for water crossings are among the complicating factors.

Preparation

Winter travel by foot requires particular types of trip preparation, safety and self-rescue considerations, clothing, gear, food, and arrangements for drinking water. Snowshoes, crampons, trekking poles with snow baskets, and other winter gear—and skill in their use—are essential for winter mountain travel.

Hike in a group of persons experienced in winter hiking. There must be multiple people in a party with such experience in the event that a leader has a mishap. *Complete a course in winter mountain safety, including cold-weather wilderness first aid.*

Confirm Current Conditions

Consult with a knowledgeable source about current conditions. Perhaps start with an outfitter or outdoor store in the region or contact the Chamber of Commerce. Pursue this inquiry to get the information you need. I do not hike in winter without a reliable forecast.

Route Finding

Route finding may be difficult as snow hides footpaths and covers cairns, blazes, and even trail signs. Ice and deep snow may make what are straightforward routes in summer dangerous to follow. Subzero wind-chill temperatures are common, as are whiteouts, when visibility may be reduced to only a few feet. Limited daylight adds to the complexities. *Navigation expertise is essential.*

Time on Trail

Expect hiking times to be one and a half to two times longer than warm weather times.

Winter Travel Modes

Standard on my winter hikes are snowshoes with built-in crampons and boot crampons—sized to fit my winter boots. When terrain is suitable, I begin my approach on backcountry skis and switch to snowshoes as the terrain steepens, stashing the skis to retrieve on the return. Crampons are essential at high elevations, where ice may render snowshoes useless. *Boot traffic alone (without snowshoes or allowable skis) may not be permitted on ski trails.*

Hikers may arrive at a trailhead to find the route packed by previous hikers such that snowshoes do not appear to be needed. Be aware that previous parties may not have reached the summit! Deep or drifted snow may necessitate snowshoe use on high ground.

Permits for Winter Hiking

Access considerations in winter depend upon whether your hikes are planned for the three peaks in Baxter State Park or the eleven peaks located elsewhere.

Baxter State Park (North Brother, Hamlin, Katahdin): BSP has a reservation and permit system specific to winter use. Contact park authorities well in advance of a proposed trip, as there are winter parties in the park virtually every day of the winter season, and bunkhouse space—the most desirable in winter—goes fast.

The other eleven peaks are available to be hiked either without a permitting process or with a day-pass policy.

- Grafton Notch State Park (Old Speck): Day-use fee has a seasonal self-pay station at the Highway 26 parking area, but there is no fee outside the summer hiking season.

- Sugarloaf Ski Area (Sugarloaf Mountain, Spaulding): Uphill access by snowshoes or permitted skis is welcome by Trail Pass ($10 per person, at Guest Services). Hikers are restricted to designated routes and time periods. Dogs not permitted. Details: www.sugarloaf.com.

- Saddleback Ski Area (Saddleback, The Horn): Winter uphill use on snowshoes or permitted skis is welcome. Access requires purchase of an uphill trail pass ($15.00) at the Ticket Office and travel on designated routes during specified hours. Dogs not permitted. Details: https://saddlebackmaine.com.

Approach Roads and Parking

Many approach roads and parking areas are not plowed. Distances to be covered to reach a trailhead from a suitable parking location will add many miles to a hike. For some locations a shuttle service may be the most practical way to access a trailhead.

Status of approach roads and trailhead parking areas as plowed or unplowed may vary from year to year. I advise calling ahead to determine current conditions. Even if snowplowing is conducted, the remote locations of many trailheads may cause them to have a low priority after a winter storm, and they may not be plowed for many days.

Peak-by-Peak Access

Old Speck

- AT South: The trailhead parking lot in Grafton Notch State Park is plowed. Snowbank accumulation may reduce available parking space. For current conditions, call Grafton Notch State Park (207-824-2912). The summit observation platform ladder may be ice covered. If so, enjoy fine views to the north and east from the clearing at the base of the tower. Nearby summit firs provide a windbreak on cold days.

Saddleback Range

- AT North: The Highway 4 AT parking lot 9.0 miles south of Rangeley is not plowed in winter. Roadside parking on Highway 4 is unsafe, as the trailhead is at a downhill curve. Snowplows may be working on the highway at any time of the day or night, including non-snow days when crews plow the snow-banks back to make room for accumulation from the next storm. Winter parties may be dropped off here and picked up at an arranged time; however, cell phone service may be limited, and pinpointing a pickup time may be difficult. I have snowshoe-hiked the AT North route to Saddleback, and it has much to recommend it if shuttle arrangements can be made.

- Fly Rod Crosby Trail (FRCT) to AT North: Another option is to park at the Saddleback ski area lodge parking lot and walk 0.4 mile up the Rock Pond Road to the trailhead for the Rock Pond and Fly Rod Crosby Trails. On snowshoes (or backcountry skis), follow FRCT markers past Rock Pond, first on an old road, subsequently a woods trail, and finally a multiuse route (snow-mobile, ATV, and foot traffic) to the AT crossing near Eddy Pond. Turn left, AT North, to ascend Saddleback and to continue to The Horn (if desired). Return by backtracking to Saddleback, then to the knob 0.2 mile AT South, where a prominent cairn and signpost (but no sign) mark the junction with the foot trail leading northwest to the ski trail route down to the Saddleback ski area lodge and parking lot. I like this itinerary because I am able to see Eddy Pond in winter and ascend Saddleback by a hike on a considerable portion of the AT without the parking or shuttle issues associated with Highway 4.

- Berry Picker's Trail: Approach roads are private and may not be plowed, depending upon owner activity. The Berry Picker's trailhead may be reached by skis via Interconnected Trail System (ITS) 89 North, which crosses the Reeds Mill Road in Madrid, 5.0 miles east of Highway 4, 100 yards past the bridge over Orbeton Stream. There is room for one or two vehicles at this road/trail junction. This is a long approach of about 7.5 miles from Reeds Mill Road to the Berry Picker's trailhead.

- Saddleback Ski Trail route: The Saddleback Mountain Road to the Saddle-back ski area is plowed in winter, providing vehicle access to the ski trail route to Saddleback summit and on to The Horn via the AT. Park in designated parking areas only. Uphill Pass required ($15 at Ticket Office); designated routes and time frames.

Mt. Abraham

- Mt. Abraham–Rapid Stream trailhead: The West Kingfield Road is plowed in winter by the town of Kingfield. Plowing on the Rapid Stream Road may depend upon timber harvest operations or private plowing patterns by local private owners. Even so, hikers should not expect plowing all the way to the summer trailhead. Vehicles must be parked so as not to block any portion of a plowed road. Logging operation vehicles and equipment may use the road at any hour of the day or night. For road conditions and plowing information, contact the Kingfield Town Office (207-265-4637).

Redington and Crocker Ranges

- Redington, South Crocker, and North Crocker from Caribou Pond Road: Typically, the Caribou Pond Road is not plowed in winter. It may be plowed for purposes of timber harvesting, Sugarloaf ski area use, or other private owner access. In those cases, public access may still not be available or may be limited. For information on winter road conditions, contact Town of Carrabassett Valley (207-237-2645), Carrabassett Valley Police (207-237-7000), or Sugarloaf ski area (207-237-2000). If the road is not plowed, there is a 4.4-mile hike (8.8 miles RT) from Highway 27 to reach the AT/Caribou Pond Road intersection. However, vehicles may not be left along Highway 27 and may not block the Caribou Pond Road, plowed or unplowed. Hikers may consider a drop-off and pickup arrangement, using personal vehicles or a shuttle. Contact the Carrabassett/Sugarloaf numbers above or Maine's Northwestern Mountains Information Center (207-235-6008) for shuttle resources and off-site parking suggestions.

Spaulding and Sugarloaf

- Spaulding, Sugarloaf from Caribou Pond Road: A hike to Sugarloaf or Spaulding from the Caribou Pond Road requires a ford of the South Branch of the Carrabassett River. Such a crossing in winter could be dangerous, if it is possible at all. I do not advise it. Instead, approach via the Sugarloaf alpine ski slope (pass required).

- North Crocker, Highway 27 trailhead, Wyman Township: Parking lot is not plowed. Parking along Highway 27 is not advised, as snowplows may operate at any time, including in good weather, when plows push back existing banks to make space for the next snowfall. A shuttle is advised.

- Sugarloaf from north—ski trail routes: Sugarloaf Access Road is plowed. This road links Highway 27 with the Sugarloaf complex. On winter weekends and other busy periods, parking lots fill quickly. A free shuttle operates from outlying lots to the base lodge area.

- Sugarloaf allows winter uphill access but, for safety purposes, requires an Uphill Pass, available at the Guest Services office for a fee ($10 per person), and designates hiking routes and allowable time frames. Passes may not be issued during bad weather or when there is other use planned for the trails designated for hiking.

Bigelow Range

- South side, Stratton Brook Pond Road trailhead: The road is plowed 0.1 mile for use by residents of the local settlement of year-round and seasonal homes.

Shuttle advised. From this point to the Stratton Brook trailhead kiosk for the Fire Warden Trail is 1.6 miles (3.2 miles RT). The snow-covered road is often traveled by snowmobiles. It is essentially level ground to the trailhead, thereby suitable for skis for this road portion of the route, when conditions are right.

- North side, Safford Brook trailhead by East Flagstaff Road: The East Flagstaff Road into the Bigelow Preserve is usually plowed, but the distance the road is cleared may vary from year to year. One pattern is for plowing to extend 1.0 mile on the road to a point 0.1 mile beyond the AT crossing and trailhead for Little Bigelow Mountain. The road beyond this point is used as a snowmobile trail for a route that goes to Round Barn and beyond to Stratton Village. A sizable parking area is plowed to provide for snowmobile trailer parking. Cross-country skiers and those on snowshoe also use this parking area and snow-packed snowmobile route.

- In some years plowing extends only to the Bog Brook Road, 0.8 mile on the East Flagstaff Road from Long Falls Dam Road, where the snow is usually pushed far enough in the direction of the East Flagstaff Road to create parking space. Bog Brook Road runs north for 0.3 mile to a small housing settlement by Flagstaff Lake. *Do not park in this settlement or in any way block the road to the settlement.* Plowing crews may operate any time of the day or night.

- The way to the Safford Brook Trail trailhead is over the unplowed portion of the East Flagstaff Road, about 4.5 to 5.0 miles, depending upon the plowing pattern for a given year. The road has a series of hills, which make for climbing and swift downhill runs. I am alert for snowmobiles on this road, wearing a bright-colored outer layer and a headlamp in low light. I keep to one side of the trail and have my party travel in single file. On tight turns I move to the outside of the turn in order not to surprise a snowmobiler coming from the opposite direction.

- The trailhead (sign) is on the left side of what would be the Round Barn parking area in summer. (Another Safford Brook Trail sign is on the north side, but this is a short section that leads 0.3 mile to the edge of Flagstaff Lake.)

- The road at the near end of the parking area is a driveway to Bigelow Lodge, a large, alpine-style building constructed in the 1970s in anticipation of the Bigelow Range becoming the site of a ski resort—a project never realized. Maine voters chose in a statewide referendum to purchase the Bigelow Range lands and create the Bigelow Preserve. During some winters the Maine Bureau of Parks and Lands (MBPL) opens this building as a day-use warming center on winter weekends and during the week of Presidents Day in February. MBPL personnel build a fire in the stone fireplace and provide hot water for coffee and tea. For information, call Bigelow Lodge (207-778-8231; 207-287-4957).

Immediate approach roads to Baxter State Park and its Perimeter Road are not plowed. Hiking parties must travel on snow to reach the park and, once there, trek to the chosen trailhead. Given the distances involved, a hike involves one or more overnight stays. Some snowmobile travel is permitted on the Perimeter Road, subject to park rules.

There are cross-country ski trails in the park. The Perimeter Road may be skied, shared with snowmobile use. Trails to the three 4,000-Footers are not groomed for skiing.

Contact Baxter State Park for information about winter rules, the permit process for winter, and winter access routes particular to your trailhead of choice (https://baxterstatepark.org; 207-723-5140).

Fishing Maine's 4,000-Footers

Maine is world famous for its brook trout fishery. To fish Maine's 4,000-Footers is to pursue the 4,000-Footer list in a unique way. Remote ponds, lakes, and streams with brook trout populations may be found on or near trails to Maine's 4,000-Footers. For fishing information, maps, and regulations, see https://maine.gov.

River and stream fishing may be best in the spring before water levels subside. Pond fishing may be productive throughout the legal fishing season.

Maps

Maps of fishing waters and details about each fishery are available online. Search for "Maine Department of Inland Fisheries and Wildlife"; click on "Lake Survey Maps." Search by the name of the pond, lake, river, or stream, followed by Maine (e.g., "Horns Pond Maine").

Licenses

Fishing in Maine requires a license from the Maine Department of Inland Fisheries and Wildlife. License fees help to sustain these precious fisheries—which include brook trout, blue-backed trout, land-locked salmon, and other species. Licenses may be purchased at sporting goods shops, outfitters, municipal offices, and online at https://maine.gov.

There are two license-free fishing days per year, one in June, the other in February. Equipment regulations and bag limits still apply. The purpose of these days is to welcome newcomers to the sport, particularly children and youth. For details, see https://maine.gov.

Maine Inland Fisheries Law Book

This essential resource for Maine inland fishing is available online (https://maine .gov) and at outlets where fishing licenses are sold. A new edition of *Maine Fishing Laws* (referred to locally as "the law book") is issued every year. Use only a current book. Regulations change.

The book describes regulations for all fishable inland waters in Maine—either by listing waters with specific per-body-of-water regulations or by indicating what waters fall under fishing general law. Even adjacent waters may have different regulations.

Many of these waters are fly-fishing only (FFO) or artificial lures only (ALO). To determine what qualifies as FFO and ALO, consult *Maine Fishing Laws* to avoid a violation. Having fishing gear in your possession may be legally construed as fishing, whether you are in the act of fishing or not.

Obtain the current *Maine Fishing Laws*, give it a close read—and enjoy the fishing!

Old Speck

- Speck Pond: 1.1 mile south of Old Speck; highest-elevation pond in Maine (3,429 feet)

Saddleback and The Horn

- Sandy River Ponds: 1.0 mile north of AT crossing on Highway 4, 8.0 miles south of Rangeley
- Eddy Pond: 3.8 miles from Highway 4 on AT North toward Saddleback
- Orbeton Stream: AT crossing, 6.1 miles north of The Horn, 6.1 miles south of Spaulding Mountain spur trail

Mt. Abraham

- Rapid Stream: By Rapid Stream Road approach to trailhead

Crocker Range and Redington

- Caribou Pond: Reached by the so-called valley route to Redington Mountain—not the South Crocker herd path. Pond in Caribou Valley, 2.9 miles north of Yellow Gate trailhead, 2.5 miles north of AT crossing of Caribou Pond Road, 0.1 mile west of the repaired beam bridge (cross the bridge) over South Branch of the Carrabassett River. This is a wild trout fishery. Protect the fish population!
- South Branch, Carrabassett River: Parallels Caribou Pond Road

Bigelow Range—Avery and West Peaks

- Stratton Brook and Stratton Brook Pond: South side of Bigelow Range; reached at beginning of Fire Warden Trail 0.4 mile from trailhead kiosk on Stratton Brook Pond Road
- Horns Pond: Reached by Fire Warden and Horns Pond Trails and AT
- Flagstaff Lake: North of Bigelow Range, 0.3 mile north of Safford Brook Trail trailhead

Baxter State Park: North Brother, Hamlin, and Katahdin

Multiple waters include Nesowadnehunk Stream, Daicey Pond, and Kidney Pond to the west, Sandy Stream Pond and a basin pond in the east, and Russell Pond and Wassataquoik Stream to the north. No fishing in Chimney Pond, Lake Cowles, or Davis Pond. The park publishes a list of fishable waters and the species therein.

The Hiker Box: Appendices

A hiker box is part of long-distance hiking culture. Find these at hiker hostels, out-fitter stores, or town information centers. The box itself may be constructed from wood specifically for its hiker purpose but more likely is a repurposed trunk, crate, or cardboard carton.

In the box are items of practical use that hikers leave for other hikers to take with them or that local people provide as gifts to hikers. What follows here is less tangible than the contents of most hiker boxes but still potentially useful.

Appendix A

Maine 4,000-Footers by Elevation

Add your summit date and notes.

Peak	Elevation	Date Summited	Notes
Katahdin	5,268 feet		
Hamlin Peak	4,756 feet		
Sugarloaf	4,250 feet		
North Crocker	4,228 feet		
Old Speck	4,170 feet		
North Brother	4,151 feet		
West Peak	4,145 feet		
Saddleback	4,120 feet		
Avery Peak	4,090 feet		
Mt. Abraham	4,050 feet		
South Crocker	4,050 feet		
The Horn	4,041 feet		
Redington	4,010 feet		
Spaulding	4,010 feet		

Appendix B
Four-Thousand-Footer Club

The Four-Thousand-Footer Club (FTFC) was formed in 1957 as an initiative of the Appalachian Mountain Club (AMC) to encourage hikers to explore White Mountain regions outside the popular Presidential and Franconia Ranges. The FTFC later expanded its vision to include all 4,000-Footers in New England, thereby adding peaks from Maine and Vermont. That list now totals sixty-seven peaks. Still more lists, with certificates to be awarded to those who complete them, have followed. Hikers who wish to qualify for the FTFC should contact the club for the official lists, rules, and application process.

As hiker interest and ambition has grown, the FTFC has developed more hiker incentives. One of the latest is the Four-Season White Mountain Four-Thousand-Footer Club for those who summit the forty-eight New Hampshire peaks in all four seasons, for a total of 192 ascents, and volunteer for forty-eight hours of trail work. That program has not yet extended to Maine (or Vermont), but hikers may certainly embrace the concept by applying the criteria to Maine. Hike the Maine peaks in all four seasons, for a total of fifty-six summits. Contact the Maine Appalachian Trail Club (MATC) or AMC to volunteer.

FTFC information: https://amc4000footer.org

Current FTFC lists include the following:
- White Mountains of New Hampshire 4,000-Footers
- White Mountains of New Hampshire 4,000-Footers in Winter
- Four-Season White Mountain Four-Thousand-Footer Club
- New England 4,000-Footers
- New England 4,000-Footers in Winter
- New England Hundred Highest: 4,000-Footers and the thirty-three next highest peaks in New England
- Northeast 111: New England and New York, in conjunction with the Adirondack 46ers

Appendix C

Keepers of the Trails: Trail-Maintaining Organizations Mentioned in This Book

Contact these organizations for specific trail information and to volunteer for trail work, assist in public education, or advocate for public lands. All these organizations have strongly supportive volunteer communities, from spirited trail maintainers to those who help with publications. Become a trail volunteer!

Appalachian Mountain Club

The Appalachian Mountain Club (AMC) maintains the Appalachian Trail (AT) in Maine from the New Hampshire border to Grafton Notch, including the Old Speck Trail (which coincides with the AT) and the Eyebrow Trail in Grafton Notch. The AMC was founded in 1876, has chapters in the Northeast and Mid-Atlantic states, maintains an extensive trail network in the White Mountains of New Hampshire and elsewhere, and publishes maps and guidebooks. In Maine the club also maintains backcountry lodges in the vicinity of the Barren-Chairback Range. The Four-Thousand-Footer Club is an initiative of the AMC. See https://www.outdoors.org.

Appalachian Trail Conservancy

The Appalachian Trail Conservancy (ATC) is not a local trail-maintaining organization as such. Rather, the organization's mission is to manage and conserve the Appalachian Trail, including coordination of the efforts of thirty-one trail-maintaining organizations, consisting largely of volunteers, in the fourteen states through which the AT passes. It is headquartered in Harpers Ferry, West Virginia. There is a seasonal regional ATC center in Monson, Maine. The ATC is a source for maps, guidebooks, first-person accounts of AT hikes, and other publications of interest to hikers. See http://appalachiantrail.org.

Baxter State Park

Baxter State Park (BSP) is a land of exceptional wild beauty and the location of three of Maine's 4,000-foot peaks: Katahdin, Hamlin, and North Brother. BSP maintains trails to the above peaks and to more than three dozen others. Magnificent lakes, wild streams, and remote ponds are within its boundaries, with trails leading to most of them.

At 230,000 acres, BSP is one of the largest state parks in the nation. It was formed largely through the extraordinary donation of the land by former Maine governor Percival Baxter, who purchased large tracts of land for the purpose of creating the park. BSP has particular rules of use as stipulated in donation covenants established by

Governor Baxter. Much of the park is a wildlife preserve. *Hence, pets are not permitted.* Park roads are made of gravel and are kept essentially in their condition at the time of donation. The speed limit is 20 mph and is strictly enforced. All camping is by permit and in designated sites. There is no wild or bivouac camping allowed. The number of vehicles allowed in the park is limited. *Advance vehicle parking reservations are advised.* Some would-be hikers are turned away at the entrance gate because all available parking spaces are filled.

Prospective visitors should contact the park early in the planning process (207-723-5140; https://baxterstatepark.org).

Friends of Baxter State Park

Friends of BSP is a spirited organization of people who serve as volunteers, provide public education, and advocate for the park, with particular attention to welcoming youth to discover Baxter State Park. See https://friendsofbaxter.org.

Maine Appalachian Trail Club

This trail-maintaining club oversees 234 miles of the AT from Grafton Notch to Baxter State Park and 60 miles of side trails to the AT all along its Maine route. The club also maintains forty lean-tos and tent sites. Significant trail maintenance is the work of volunteers, who come from Maine and across the country. See http://matc.org.

Maine Huts and Trails

Maine Huts and Trails (MHT) operates four backcountry lodges, 60 miles of connecting trail, and additional miles of side trails. The Stratton Brook Hut is located south of the Bigelow Preserve on Oak Knoll with a view of Bigelow Range from the south. Flagstaff Hut is by the east shore of Flagstaff Lake, north of the Bigelow Range.

Although not on immediate access trails to Avery and West Peaks, the MHT huts have been used by some hikers as a base camp for such hikes. For trail system and lodging information and rates, contact MHT (https://mainehuts.org).

Maine Bureau of Parks and Lands (MBPL)

The Maine Bureau of Parks and Lands (MBPL) manages the Bigelow Preserve, location of Avery Peak and West Peak (and thousands of acres of other public lands in the state). It coordinates trail maintenance with the MATC for preserve trails described in this book. See https://maine.gov.

Appendix D

Trail Towns for Supplies, Gear, Food, Lodging, and Local Information

Old Speck

Bethel

Bethel is well situated between the Maine section of the White Mountain National Forest and the Mahoosuc Range and welcomes day and long-distance hikers. The Sunday River ski area and regional Nordic ski venues are major winter attractions that host summer events such as trail running, mountain biking, and, of course, hiking. Gear shops, lodging, restaurants, grocery stores, and shuttle services are available. Downtown Bethel is 16 miles from the Old Speck trailhead in Grafton Notch.

- Bethel Chamber of Commerce: https://bethelmaine.com.

Saddleback Mountain and The Horn

Rangeley

In the heart of the Rangeley Lakes Region, ringed by mountain peaks, Rangeley has been a center for outdoor pursuits for generations. Percival Baxter, who donated the land for what is now Baxter State Park, spent many an outdoor season here, fishing and hunting. Rangeley is an Appalachian Trail Community and a key stop for paddlers on the 742-mile Northern Forest Canoe Trail from Old Forge, New York, to Fort Kent, Maine.

Here, find outdoor gear stores with hiking supplies and clothing, grocery stores and restaurants, lodging of many kinds, shuttle services, a bookstore, and fishing-supply shops.

- The Rangeley Lakes Heritage Trust is a regional organization that maintains a network of trails and a campground, and it is a key source for trail information. The trust maintains a year-round information center in downtown Rangeley: http://rlht.org.
- Rangeley Lakes Chamber of Commerce: https://rangeleymaine.com.
- A new welcome center/visitor kiosk in Madrid on Highway 4 by the Reeds Mill Road junction is in the planning stage. Information on hiker services, outdoor recreation of many kinds, and maps for trails in the region south and north of the Saddleback Range will be available.

Mt. Abraham, Spaulding, Sugarloaf, North and South Crocker, Redington, Avery Peak, and West Peak

Four Highway 27 communities serve this region of eight 4,000-Footers: Kingfield, Carrabassett Valley, Sugarloaf Village at the Sugarloaf ski area, and Stratton Village in the town of Eustis. For the north and east slopes of the Bigelow Range, the nearest community is the village of North New Portland, 7.5 miles east of Kingfield on Highway 16. Farmington, county seat for Franklin County, is a major service center 40 to 45 miles south of the peaks listed.

Information Center: Maine's Northwestern Mountain

The regional information center for visitors, located north of Kingfield on Highway 27 in Carrabassett Valley, adopted a new name in 2019: "Maine's Northwestern Mountains." It is staffed in person year-round, with hours varying by season. The center has hiker services information for the above four communities along the Highway 27 corridor. An outdoor kiosk with maps and flyers for many local services is accessible twenty-four hours a day at the center. See http://mainesnorthwestern mountains.com.

Kingfield

Kingfield is an Appalachian Trail Community. The town has a lively arts community with local galleries, frequent concerts—including an annual summer concert by the Bangor Symphony—and a seasonal Friday-night "Arts Walk." Services include lodging, grocery stores, restaurants, a pharmacy, an outdoor-clothing store, and an outdoor-gear store. A hiker shuttle service is available.

Kingfield is headquarters for Maine Huts and Trails, which maintains a network of four backcountry lodges with overnight accommodations, hot showers, and guided events. Some hikers approach the Bigelow Preserve and Avery and West Peaks from the Stratton Brook Hut. Flagstaff Hut is a potential staging site for a Bigelow Range hike. Shuttle information is available. See https://mainehuts.org.

Sugarloaf Village and Carrabassett Valley

Carrabassett Valley lies immediately north of Kingfield on Highway 27. "Carrabassett" is an Abenaki term meaning "place where moose cross." The centerpiece of recreational, cultural, and economic activity in this region is Sugarloaf ski area, which is home to a year-round village on the mountain, homes and condominium units, a golf course, and a fitness center. The village complex has lodging, restaurants, and clothing and gear shops. The nearby Sugarloaf Outdoor Center is a year-round locale for hiking, mountain biking, snowshoeing, and Nordic ski events. The Sugarloaf ski area hosts national and international competitions in snow sports. Many village businesses are open year-round. The busiest season is winter, as one might expect.

There is no downtown area as such for the town of Carrabassett Valley. Along a 6.0-mile stretch of Highway 27, south of the Sugarloaf Access Road, lie lodgings, restaurants, small grocery stores, and two gas stations—one with mechanic services. Hiker shuttle service is available.

Stratton Village, Eustis

Stratton Village is 5.0 miles north of the Highway 27 trailhead in Wyman Township, 4.4 miles north of Stratton Brook Pond Road to the Bigelow Preserve, and 7.5 miles north of the Sugarloaf Access Road. A common resupply stop for Appalachian Trail hikers and a Northern Forest Canoe Trail community, Stratton has lodging, restaurants, grocery stores, and shuttle services. A general store has some camping items. The Dead River Historical Society, open during summer months, has rare information about the Benedict Arnold expedition to Quebec City in 1775 and the removal of the residents of the Flagstaff, Dead River, and Bigelow communities in 1949 to make way for the new Long Falls Dam and consequent flooding of the Dead River Valley to form Flagstaff Lake.

North New Portland Village

This village has a grocery store/diner that serves a fine breakfast and is the last stop in the area for supplies. The nearest gas station is in Kingfield.

Farmington

Farmington, population 7,500, county seat of Franklin County, is the largest town in the wider region, with lodging, restaurants, supermarkets, coffee shops, pharmacies, vehicle-repair services, two bookstores, hardware stores, and retailers carrying hiking footwear, hiking clothing, and camping gear. United States Geological Survey (USGS) topographic maps are available at the US Department of Agriculture Soil and Water Conservation Office, Park Street, Monday to Friday, 8:00 a.m. to 4:00 p.m.

Franklin Memorial Hospital, the regional medical center, is here, as is the University of Maine at Farmington. Western Maine Transportation provides bus service between some towns. Shuttle and taxi services are available. The town center is located 22 miles south of Kingfield. Contact the Franklin County Chamber of Commerce for information (https://franklincountymaine.org).

Baxter State Park

Millinocket is the northernmost official Appalachian Trail Community along the Maine-to-Georgia Appalachian Trail, located 17.0 miles south of Baxter State Park. The headquarters of the park are here, along with restaurants, grocery stores, pharmacies, some camping-gear stores, a variety of lodging and vehicle services, and shuttle services. Millinocket Regional Hospital is the medical center. Bus service connecting to Bangor, Augusta, Portland, and Boston is available in Medway, 11.0 miles east.

The settlement of Millinocket Lake, 8.0 miles north of Millinocket, en route to BSP, has a diner, lodging, and a store with grocery items, hiker supplies, and gas. The Katahdin Chamber of Commerce can provide additional information (https://katahdinmaine.com).

Other, smaller settlements in the region offer food, lodging, and supplies. Be on the watch for homes and farms along the way with a sign out for homemade pies, local Maine honey, fresh produce, handwoven baskets, and more delights.

Appendix E
Hiker Talk: Terms of the Trail

Abenaki (also Abnaki): Native American nation or tribe, longtime dwellers of what is now Maine, New England, and eastern Canada; members of the Wabanaki Confederacy or Alliance, which also included Mi'kmaq, Maliseet, Passamaquoddy, and Penobscot tribes. Many Maine place-names are based upon terminology assigned by Abenaki, Penobscot, and other affiliated nations (e.g., *Carrabassett, Ktaadn*).

Alpine zone: In practical terms, the area above tree line. In the northeastern United States, alpine zones are located at elevations much lower than in the Rocky Mountains, the Sierras, and along the Pacific Crest. Harsh weather, with high winds, sleet and snow, fog, and icing, may occur well into the beginning of summer and appear before summer ends on Maine's 4,000-Footers. Only limited types of flora and fauna can survive such conditions.

The alpine zones on Katahdin, the Bigelow Range, the Saddleback Range, and Mt. Abraham are extensive. Smaller, even tiny, alpine niches may be found on most 4,000-Footers in Maine.

Appalachian Mountain Club (AMC): Host organization of the Four-Thousand-Footer Club. Maintains the AT in Maine between the New Hampshire border and Grafton Notch—which includes Old Speck Mountain.

Appalachian Trail North: The AT heading toward the northern terminus of the Appalachian Trail, which is Katahdin. This is *not* necessarily the compass direction north. At any given point on the AT, as the footpath winds its way, AT North may head east, west, or even south, while leading in the eventual direction of north. Signage pointing to AT North refers to the eventual direction of Katahdin.

Appalachian Trail South: The AT in the direction of the southern terminus at Springer Mountain in Georgia. For example, when hiking west on the Bigelow Range from Avery Peak to West Peak, one is on the AT South, because eventually, continuing on the trail in that direction, a hiker reaches Georgia.

AT: Appalachian Trail.

Baxter Peak: Synonymous with "Katahdin." This is the highest peak on the Katahdin massif, 5,268 feet.

Blaze: A paint strip, usually 2 inches wide by 6 inches high on trees, rocks, and posts. AT blazes are white. Blue is commonly the color on Maine public lands and on side trails connecting to the AT. (An exception is the orange-blazed Eyebrow Trail on Old Speck.)

Bushwhack: Make a way over terrain where there is no marked trail. There are two bushwhack routes in this book, both on Redington Mountain—although repeated use has created discernable *herd paths*.

Cairn: A rock pile built to mark a trail above tree line or along ledge or rocky ground where there are no trees for paint blazes.

Col: Low point between two peaks. Lengthy cols in the Northeast may be called saddles.

Deciduous: Trees that drop leaves in fall. Synonymous with hardwood, with a few exceptions. The larch is a softwood tree with needles, but these needles turn a yellow-orange color and drop in the fall season. Therefore it is a deciduous conifer!

Distance: Length in miles (occasionally in feet or yards) between two points. In this book distances are always a good-faith estimate. I have consulted a variety of reputable sources for the trails herein and seek to provide the most accurate information currently available. However, different methods have been used over the years to measure distance. Books, maps, and signs take some time to be updated. When there are discrepancies, they are not large.

Down-climbing: Turning 180 degrees to face the slope on a steep downward section and let oneself down backward one step at a time. This places the center of gravity closer to the slope and may reduce chances of a fall. Particularly in order on very steep terrain and when wearing a heavy pack.

Draw: Small ravine; may be a perennial or seasonal watercourse.

Dry-ki: Deadwood washed up on a downwind shore of a lake or pond or at a stream outlet.

Elevation gain: Cumulative elevation gained along the length of a given trail or route, from trailhead to summit. This figure is an estimate, because an ascending trail may drop into a draw or col before resuming an upward course. For example, a hiker who ascends Avery Peak and then West Peak on the same hike, after summiting Avery, loses elevation in the descent to Avery Col, then gains elevation to reach the top of West Peak. For this reason, "elevation gain" and another term, "prominence," are not quite the same. To avoid confusion, I limit the use of "prominence" in this book.

Erratic: Boulder moved by glacial activity, from hundreds of feet up to many miles. Frequent sight in the Maine mountains, including on ridgetops.

Felsenmeer: Literally a sea of rock; extensive area of rock rubble in an alpine zone. Largest areas of felsenmeer in Maine are on the Katahdin Tableland and on the main and middle peaks of Mt. Abraham. Considered the effect of the freeze-thaw cycle.

Ford: To cross a stream where there is no bridge. Hikers are advised to obtain instruction in safe fording technique. This includes wearing sturdy, good-grip footwear and unclipping pack belts and loosening straps in order to jettison a pack in the event of a fall. How to cross in a group, how to use trekking poles when fording, and how to assist a hiker who falls are among other skills essential to practice and master before fording a stream. Even at low depth, mountain streams can destabilize a hiker—suddenly.

Potentially dangerous fords include Orbeton Stream between the Saddleback Range and Spaulding Mountain; Carrabassett River by the Caribou Pond Road; and Wassataquoik Stream, Baxter Park. Any stream may rise to risky levels from storms or seasonal runoff. Those who through-hike the AT in Maine en route to hike all 4,000-Footers will encounter many potential fords. *It is advised to obtain instruction in fording technique before pursuing the hikes in this book.*

Four-point hiking or climbing: Using hands and feet to ascend—or descend—a steep section of trail.

Hardwood: Synonymous with deciduous; trees that release leaves in the fall season. Although the wood of hardwoods tends to be harder than that of softwoods, some hardwood trees, such as aspen, have a softer wood than some so-called softwoods.

Herd path: A route worn by hiker use over time. Herd paths do not ordinarily have signs, cairns, blazes, or other reliable markings and are not maintained by a trail organization. Also known as a "social trail." There are two herd paths in this book, both leading to Redington Mountain.

The alpine ski trail route to Saddleback might be considered a herd path in its final 0.1 mile below the ridge. Signs and blazes once along this route have become so weather-beaten as to be indistinguishable. However, there is a discernable worn path along much of the route.

Hike your own hike: To hike at one's own pace, on one's own schedule, with one's own on-trail interests (e.g., flora and fauna, geology, photography, etc.) and otherwise not to be in competition with other hikers. May also mean to choose gear, clothing, and food without comparing oneself to others.

Example: Some 4,000-Footer hikers aim to complete the list in the shortest possible time, often hiking multiple peaks on the same day. Others prefer to spread hikes over many occasions, spending extended time on trail for observation of wildlife, trees, wildflowers, and wetlands. Other examples: Hiking a given peak every month of the year or hiking every trail that approaches a peak are among the alternative ways hikers have pursued the 4,000-Footer list.

Interconnected Trail System (ITS): Network of snowmobile trails in Maine and the Northeast.

Katahdin: Abenaki and Penobscot term for "highest mountain" or "greatest mountain." To Native people, this was more than a geographic descriptor. Such high ground has deep spiritual significance. It is to be approached with quiet reverence and with respect for all forms of life to be found here—birds, mammals large and small, alpine flowers, grasses, sedge, mosses.

Perhaps originally pronounced *Ktaadn* by people of the Penobscot Nation, the term is synonymous with Baxter Peak. It also has been applied to the entire mountain massif rising from the surrounding stream and river valleys, including Baxter Peak, South Peak, the Knife Edge, Chimney Peak, Pamola Peak, Hamlin Peak, the North Peaks, and the tableland.

Although the term "Mt. Katahdin" is in frequent use, the original Native American term already implies mount or mountain, and therefore "mount" as part of the name of the mountain is redundant. Baxter State Park staff tend to use the sole term "Katahdin."

Krummholz: Stunted tree growth near or above tree line; balsam fir, white birch, and black spruce are common krummholz trees.

Lean-to: A three-sided log or wood frame structure with an open front. The term derives from traditional makeshift temporary shelters constructed by leaning branches and boughs against a crosspiece lashed to two trees. Contemporary lean-tos have a broad-planked sleeping platform. Also called a shelter. AT lean-tos are provided for through-hikers as priority users because many of them do not carry tents and depend on lean-tos for shelter.

Leave no trace: The practice of carrying all waste out of the wilderness setting. Also of not trampling vegetation on or off trail, not marking trees or peeling bark, and not removing artifacts of any kind. It includes burying human and dog waste or packing it out, which is now required—and enforced—in certain US wilderness areas.

Light and fast: To pack only the minimal gear and supplies required for safety, reasonable comfort, and proper nutrition, thereby, with reduced load, having the potential to move quickly. Light-and-fast standards include capacity for self-rescue and incorporate the Ten Essentials.

Maine's High Peaks: Discontinued branding term formerly, and variously, applied to the region bordered by Rangeley, Stratton, the northern end of the Bigelow Range, and Kingfield, where ten of Maine's 4,000-Footers are located. Some publications treat the Saddleback Range as separate; others treat the Bigelow Range as separate. In 2019, the Flagstaff Area Business Association formally changed the term to "Maine's Northwestern Mountains."

Maine's Northwestern Mountains: Branding term that replaced Maine's High Peaks, effective 2019.

Massif: From French, a mountain mass, extensive high ground that is home to multiple peaks. In this book, used occasionally in reference to Katahdin and to Sugarloaf.

No-cook: Approach to meal planning and preparation whereby trail meals do not require cooking. Hikers choose no-cook to save carrying the weight of cooking gear and fuel.

North, south, east, west: Sometimes referred to in this book as compass north and so forth. The general compass direction. Example: A view north may include the general direction from northwest to northeast. Different from *Appalachian Trail North* and *Appalachian Trail South*.

Peak-bagging: Various meanings include (1) hiking 4,000-Footers with the goal of summiting all of them ("I am out to peak-bag Maine's 4,000-Footers this summer"); (2) hiking multiple peaks in one day ("We plan to peak-bag North Crocker and South Crocker on the same day"); and (3) hiking with the intent of reaching the summit in the shortest amount of elapsed time.

Penobscot: The nation of Native Americans closely associated with the Katahdin region, whose term *Ktaadn* informed the name now widely used for Maine's highest mountain. The Penobscot people, and other Native American nations in Maine and beyond, regard *Ktaadn* with respect and reverence and call on visitors to do the same.

Pitch: A steep drop on trail that usually requires some combination of four-point hiking, scrambling, or down-climbing.

Prominence: The difference in elevation between two adjacent peaks or the elevation difference from a trailhead to the summit. To qualify as a 4,000-Footer, if two peaks over 4,000 feet are adjacent, the difference between the lowest point in a connecting col must be at least 200 feet below both summits for both to qualify. For this reason, South Peak on Katahdin, elevation 5,260 feet, does not qualify because the difference in elevation between South Peak and adjacent Baxter Peak (5,268 feet), which sit on a contiguous ridge, is only 28 feet. Similarly, the North Peaks (a.k.a. Howe Peaks) in Baxter State Park, lying north of Hamlin Peak, do not qualify because the cols between them and the col between Hamlin Peak and these North Peaks do not meet the 200-foot elevation standard. To avoid confusion between this term and "elevation gain," I rarely use "prominence" in this book.

Rock-hop: There are two different meanings: (1) on fragile ground above tree line and elsewhere, to step from rock to rock to avoid crushing or otherwise disturbing alpine flowers, moss, and other sensitive growth; (2) on stream crossings, to step from rock to rock instead of wading, when rock positions make this possible. In both cases, the advised movement is a series of deliberate steps—not hops.

Rungs: Iron bars attached to steep sections of rock to provide hand- and/or footholds. There are rungs on the Eyebrow Trail route to Old Speck, on the AT approach to Saddleback from Maine Highway 4 (above Eddy Pond), and on the Hunt Trail (AT) to Katahdin below the Gateway.

Scrambling: Moving up a steep section of trail by using hands and feet. Also known as four-point hiking or close climbing.

Self-rescue capacity: The knowledge and skill set to care for an injured or ill person in a wilderness setting where and when external rescue services may not be able to reach the scene for many hours or even days. *All parties hiking 4,000-Footers are advised to have the capacity for self-rescue.*

Slow hiking: A hiker's version of taking time to smell the roses. For example, while on a 4,000-Footer hike, pausing to examine diapensia, sandwort, or reindeer lichen; a red squirrel's midden; the intriguing configuration of flag trees; or bands of fir waves. Another example would be sitting in silence on occasion to listen for the call of a Bicknell's thrush or to improve chances of seeing a pine marten or a bobcat or to notice the sound and direction of the wind. The peak still gets bagged. There is no rush.

Softwood: Coniferous (cone-bearing) trees. Examples: pine, fir, spruce, cedar, hemlock, larch.

Spur: A side trail that leads from a main trail to a peak. In this book there are spurs (trails) to Old Speck, Abraham (Abram), and Spaulding. The herd path from South Crocker might also be considered a spur, even though it is not a maintained trail, because it is an out-and-back route from the main trail (in this case, the AT) connecting South Crocker and North Crocker.

T3 R9 WELS (et al.): Township 3 Range 9 West of Eastern Line of State. Early surveys divided much of northern Maine into unnamed townships, identified by township (T) and range (R) numbers and referenced to an established boundary (e.g., Maine's eastern border) or to a particular land acquisition, usually quite large (e.g., BKP WKR refers to Bingham Kennebec Purchase, West of Kennebec River). Many towns have since acquired names that replace the original TR designation; some retain both the old and the new designations. Large parts of Maine still retain the TR moniker for unorganized townships.

Tag: To spend minimum time on a summit—reach the top, turn around, head down. Tagging is at times a necessity because of weather conditions or lateness of the day. Hikers whose primary objective is simply reaching a summit, rather than spending time exploring it, choose the tag method.

Tarn: Small pond formed by glacial activity, usually found in a sag along a ridge or at the base of a cirque.

Ten Essentials: List of gear, clothing, and specific preparations deemed essential for safe traveling in wilderness settings. Originally developed by The Mountaineers, a Seattle-based outdoor club, and published in 1974. The list has been revised over the years to consider newly available gear and updated safety protocols. Variations may be found via the internet.

Through-hike: A long, multiday, point-to-point hike. Commonly associated with AT hikers seeking to hike the full length of the trail. The term is also used by some hikers who travel only the Maine portion of the AT or other lengthy distances.

Trail running: Running on hiking trails! That is, choosing to run, rather than hike, mountain trails. In recent years, trail running has become a sport of its own. Outdoor gear manufacturers have developed trail-running shoes, day packs suited to running, and other lightweight gear. Requires careful planning in order to carry safety gear and to provide for ample intake of food and water.

Tree line: Point on a mountain where there is no tree growth, beyond low stubble or krummholz, owing to combinations of elevation, terrain, and prevailing weather conditions. Sometimes defined as terrain where trees typically do not exceed 5 feet in height.

Trekking poles: Resembling ski poles, trekking poles are used as a set of two, one in each hand, to provide purchase and stability on hiking trails. Long popular in Europe, trekking poles have gained widespread use by long-distance hikers in North America. Most are adjustable for height, have comfort grips designed for hiking, and have the option of attaching snow baskets for winter travel.

Twitch trail: A rough road on forestland, cut for—and further formed by—teams of oxen or horses hauling harvested logs on sledges or pulling them over snow or open ground. It was rarely a smooth ride, as the ground was usually sloped and rough. The teams "twitched" logs out of the woods. In an era of mechanical harvesting equipment, when skidders move logs from the woods to a log landing or yard, the term endures. A twitch trail is a route once used to haul logs.

Wilderness first aid (WFA): A body of knowledge and skills for providing first aid in scenarios commonly encountered in wilderness settings. These include, but are not limited to, hypothermia and hyperthermia, orthopedic injury, and breathing, bleeding, and cardiac emergencies. WFA certification is available through training courses offered by specifically qualified instructors. *It is advised that parties hiking 4,000-foot and higher mountains include WFA-certified hikers. A key component of self-rescue capacity is WFA certification.*

Winter conditions: Sleet, freezing rain, and snow, often accompanied by high winds. The location of the Maine mountains at the confluence of three major weather patterns (south to north; west to east; northwest to southeast) and halfway between the equator and the North Pole may result in *winter conditions in the mountains at any point in the calendar year.* Weather may change suddenly with the arrival of a front. Summiting a peak in winter conditions does not in itself qualify a hike for the winter 4,000-Footers club. See *winter season* below.

Winter season: For purposes of qualifying for the Winter New England Four-Thousand-Footer Club, a peak is to be summited in the calendar season of winter (i.e., between the moment of the winter solstice in December and the moment of the spring equinox in March) for the year when the hike is made.

Appendix F
Good Reads

Adkins, Leonard M. *Wildflowers of the Appalachian Trail*. 3rd ed. Harpers Ferry, WV: Appalachian Trail Conservancy, 2017.

Burnell, Alan L., and Kenny R. Wing. *Lost Villages of Flagstaff Lake*. Charleston, SC: Arcadia Publishing, 2010.

Chazin, Daniel D., ed. *Appalachian Trail Data Book*. Harpers Ferry, WV: Appalachian Trail Conservancy, 2020.

Dunlap, Doug. *Day Hiking in the Western Maine Mountains*. 2nd ed. Camden, ME: Down East Books, 2021.

Kish, Carey M., ed. *Maine Mountain Guide*. 11th ed. Boston: Appalachian Mountain Club, 2018.

Miller, David "Awol." *The A.T. Guide: A Handbook for Hiking the Appalachian Trail, Northbound Edition, 2021*. Wilmington, NC: ATguide.com, 2021.

Neff, John. *Katahdin: An Historic Journey*. Boston: Appalachian Mountain Club Books, 2006.

Pinkham, Steve. *Mountains of Maine: Intriguing Stories behind Their Names*. Camden, ME: Down East Books, 2009.

Slack, Nancy G., and Allison W. Bell. *Field Guide to the New England Alpine Summits*. Boston: AMC Books, 2013.

Smith, Steven D., and Mike Dickerman. *The 4000-Footers of the White Mountains*. 2nd ed. Littleton, NH: Bondcliff Books, 2017. (Third edition scheduled for 2020.)

Sylvester, Robert, ed. *Appalachian Trail Thru-Hikers Companion*. Harpers Ferry, WV: Appalachian Trail Conservancy, 2021.

Tekiela, Stan. *Birds of Maine: Field Guide*. Cambridge, MN: Adventure Publishing, 2002.

There Was a Land: Memories of Flagstaff, Dead River, and Bigelow. N.p.: Flagstaff Memorial Chapel Association, 1999. Available from Dead River Historical Society, PO Box 15, Stratton, ME 04982.

Acknowledgments

There would be no trails to hike if not for the dedicated men and women who serve in the Maine mountains as trail builders and maintainers. Most are volunteers with the Maine Appalachian Trail Club or the Appalachian Mountain Club. Some are trail crews of Baxter State Park and the Maine Bureau of Parks and Lands. Others are young adults with the Maine Conservation Corps, cheerfully wrestling with the building of bog bridges and rock staircases, water bars, and such—while creating an infrastructure to serve the hiking public for generations. While most of us are hiking the trails, they are working on them. Deep thanks to all concerned. I think of you at every chiseled rock step, paint blaze, cairn, removed blowdown, and carved wooden sign.

I have been visiting Baxter State Park, in every season, for many years and am grateful to park personnel who are always helpful with trail reports, weather reports, and mighty good advice. They clearly love what they do and the magnificent place where they do it. To the new superintendent, Eben Sypitkowski, and all park staff and volunteers go my high praise and deep appreciation.

The Bigelow Preserve and Grafton Notch State Park are managed by the men and women of the Maine Bureau of Parks and Lands—as are dozens of other parcels of public land entrusted by the people of Maine to the bureau's care-filled management. These lands are a precious part of the Maine landscape, scattered from one end of our state to the other.

There is such a thing as hiker community on the trails of the mountains of Maine—local residents, visitors from across the United States, and those who come here from every continent on earth. (I have met people on trail who have worked in Antarctica.) I have found many a person on trail to be friendly, generous with information, and ready to help with problem solving of many kinds—from a broken trekking pole to a balky camp stove to the best place in town to buy breakfast. I am grateful for this trail community, people from many walks of life, even different native languages. You, on trail, you know what I mean. I acknowledge you too.

Particular appreciation goes to Michael Steere of Down East Books, a division of Rowman & Littlefield, for his invitation to prepare this book and his counsel at key times as it took shape, and to Patricia Stevenson and other members of the Down East staff who have been helpful to me. I am grateful.

To Mary, my wife, life companion: For patience and more patience, and for loving support for this project, you have my loving appreciation. Now, let's go for a hike!